Nostalgic Memories
of
SHEFFIELD

2

The publishers would like to thank the following companies for their
support in the production of this book

Main sponsor
Cutting & Wear

Abbey Forged Products
Ancon Building Products
Arkote Ltd
Atkinson Walker (Saws) Ltd
Birkdale School
Bolton Surgical
Brook Bakery
Carrs of Sheffield
Edwin Jagger
Firth Rixson
Gripple Limited
Hadee Engineering
Hadfield Cawkwell Davidson
Johnson & Allen
JRI Orthopaedics Ltd
Lincoln Electric UK
G & M Lunt
Ponsford
Pyramid Carpets
Ronseal
Sheffield Assay Office
Shepherd Distribution Services
SIG
University of Sheffield
Wolf Safety Lamp Company

First published in Great Britain by True North Books Limited
England HX3 6SN
01422 244555
www.truenorthbooks.com

Copyright © True North Books Limited, 2012

ISBN 978 - 1906649784

Text, design and origination by True North Books
Printed and bound by Charlesworth Press

Nostalgic Memories
of
SHEFFIELD

CONTENTS

VICTORIAN & EDWARDIAN SHEFFIELD

PAGE 6

AROUND THE STREETS OF SHEFFIELD

PAGE 12

ENTERTAINMENT, LEISURE & PASTIMES

PAGE 36

BUILDINGS & MONUMENTS

PAGE 62

WORLD WAR

PAGE 76

EVENTS & OCCASIONS

PAGE 86

GETTING AROUND

PAGE 94

WORKING LIFE

PAGE 100

INTRODUCTION

'Change' is relentless and in some parts of the area the transformation will be more obvious than others. Sheffield city centre and the roads around it have changed significantly from times gone by. Some of the older and architecturally impressive buildings have retained their originality on the outside, however, their uses have changed.

The title of this new book, 'Nostalgic Memories of Sheffield', tells you all you need to know about what is captured within its pages. Turning over leaf after leaf will bring you to a treasure trove from the last century. Through the photographs, images and thoughtful text, the reader is taken on a steam train ride back through the mists of time to an age when mum would nip into Woolworths and dad could buy a suit at the Fifty Shilling Tailor. We make no apologies for the fact that some of the photographs will be outside living memory because they will still be familiar to us. They may feature an event described to us by a close relative or they could feature historical landmarks such as bridges and buildings.

Whatever the view taken on the boundaries which separate 'history', 'nostalgia' or 'the present', we should all invest a little time occasionally to reflect on the past and the people and events which helped to shape life as we know it today.

The companies and organisations that have thrived in the area, over the recent decades, are many. The Sheffield district has a proud tradition of creativity, enterprise and innovation and we take great pleasure in including in this book, histories of an outstanding selection of different companies, whose contribution to the development and sustainability of the city's economic prosperity is a matter of record. With their co-operation and access to their respective photographic archives, we have been able to tell their stories. Hopefully this will trigger the memories of local people who have worked for them, or been touched by their part in community life.

Sheffield has always been a vibrant city, buzzing with energy, but different episodes in its life can be seen here. So, think of youthful days at the old dance hall or courting in the cinemas of old and be entertained again as we revisit Nostalgic Memories of Sheffield…Happy memories!

TEXT	STEVE AINSWORTH, TONY LAX
PHOTOGRAPH RESEARCH	TONY LAX
DESIGNER	SEAMUS MOLLOY
BUSINESS DEVELOPMENT MANAGER	PETER PREST

VICTORIAN & EDWARDIAN
SHEFFIELD

Above: This very early photograph of a Sheffield street scene is dated 1885. It depicts Moorhead, looking towards Pinstone Street. T and G Roberts drapers is to the left. On the right is a public drinking fountain, whilst centre stage is an ice-cream vendor. Public drinking fountains were an important part of the Victorian street scene: clean water had not always been a normal part of life. Indeed, until the great cholera epidemic, little thought had been given to the provision of safe clean water to drink. Following the deaths of thousands in the mid 19th century, civic authorities everywhere began to pay attention, build new reservoirs, and pipe clean water from them into towns and cities for the first time since the Romans had left Britain 15 centuries earlier. Wealthy local philanthropists often paid for the individual drinking fountains.

Did you know?

The area now occupied by the City of Sheffield has been inhabited since at least the late Upper Palaeolithic period, about 12,800 years ago.

This glass plate photo of Fitzalan Square was taken over a century ago, in 1894. The cameraman is looking towards Commercial Street. On the right are the Sheffield Gas Company's offices and the Birmingham District and Counties Bank. On the left is the Haymarket General Post Office. We have rather forgotten just how important the GPO was back then for the post office dealt not just in letter and parcels but in every form of long distance communication, not least telegrams, which could instantly transmit messages across the world, and of course the new-fangled telephones. The gas lamp on the right, with its plinth to provide a seat for people to rest is a perfect example of its kind. Meanwhile, walking directly towards the camera is a very prosperous looking gentleman indeed; perhaps he is one of the owners of the gas company, or even a director of the bank.

Above: Nothing changes, it seems. Here's a corner of the outpatients 'waiting hall' at Sheffield Royal Infirmary's captured for posterity in 1897. New hospitals may have been built, and patients may be better dressed today, but folk were queuing up to be seen over a hundred years ago, and today their great-great-great grandchildren find themselves doing exactly the same thing. At least the treatment given today is far better than it was then: a few stitches and a dab of disinfectant was often all that folk could expect in 1897. There was no penicillin or other anti-biotics available in those days, indeed there were barely any useful medicines available at all. But happily anaesthetics had by then been around for fifty years or so. Having a limb sawn off was at least painless - even if the risk of gangrene or blood poisoning and subsequent death remained frighteningly high.

Left: Hunter's Bar toll bar on Ecclesall Road closed for business at midnight on 31 October, 1884. The figure in the doorway is most probably James Percy, the last lessee who paid an annual fee of £2,565 for the privilege of occupying the building and collecting the tolls. Earlier, in 1871, the gatekeeper was Jacob Thompson. His wife and two daughters lived with him. In order to raise funds for road construction and maintenance most main roads in England were toll roads or 'turnpikes' from the late 18th century onwards. Ecclesall Road was constructed in the early part of the 19th century, and was operated as a turnpike road by the Sheffield and Chapel en le Frith Trust—the first toll being paid at Hunter's Bar. The tolls were abolished in 1884 and the toll house at Hunter's Bar was demolished, although the gate posts were preserved ultimately to become a feature in the centre of Hunters Bar roundabout.

Above: The Corn Exchange, Broad Street, features here in this photo taken around the time of the First World War. Built for the Duke of Norfolk in 1881, the Central hall was destroyed by fire in 1947. The offices surrounding the exchange were demolished in 1964. In the foreground is the new Market Hotel prominently advertising Sheffield brewers Gilmour's. This was Sheffield's second largest brewer, founded in 1831. It acquired the Ladysbridge Brewery from W H Birks in 1900. Many people have been confused by Gilmour's assumption of the name 'Windsor Ales', still to be seen in the etched windows of several Sheffield pubs, and also by its use of the Windsor Castle trademark. The reason is that in the period 1902-1915 Gilmour's had control of the Windsor Brewery in Upper Parliament Street, Liverpool, although no direct connection with the Berkshire town is known.

Right: On 21 May, 1897, Queen Victoria visited the city of Sheffield. In honour of the royal visit this 'Marble Arch' was erected in Pinstone Street. St Paul's Church can be seen in the background. The reason for the Queen-Empress' visit was her Diamond Jubilee tour. Queen Victoria had come to the throne in June 1837 at the age of just 18 and was now celebrating 60 years as monarch – a jubilee not to be matched until 2012 by Queen Elizabeth II. Folk were both surprised and delighted by the Queen's visit: since the death of her husband Prince Albert in 1861 'the Old Queen' as she was widely known had spent much of her life out of the public gaze, either at Osborne House on the Isle of Wight, or at Balmoral in Scotland. The Diamond Jubilee seemed to give Victoria a new lease of life, and a renewed appetite for public appearances.

Below: Crookes is a suburb of Sheffield, about a mile and a half west of the city centre. It borders Broomhill to the south, Walkley and Crookesmoor to the east and open countryside around the River Rivelin to the north. Crookes is said to derive its name from the Old Norse 'Krkor' which means a nook or corner of land. The area was sparsely settled until the 1790s, when a turnpike road was opened from Sheffield to Glossop, running via the southern end of Crookes, spurring development of the area. By Edwardian times when this photo was taken Crookes was very much 'on the map' with the tram route having been extended there, making daily commuting into and out of the city an attractive proposition. Ten years later and this street scene would undoubtedly feature motor vehicles, but in 1905 trams were still the only serious challenge to horses.

Below: There were no cars about in South Street when this photograph was taken. And no wonder, the date is 1902 and the number of motor vehicles on the streets of Sheffield could probably have still been counted on the fingers of one hand. The building is the Punch Bowl Inn at number 140 South Street. 'Shanks Pony' was still most common means of transport for modest distances. As for transporting small loads, the hand-cart was a ubiquitous feature of the streets. The two lads in the foreground could make a steady income, at least of pocket money, shifting heavy shopping and parcels for a penny a time. Behind the boys is an ice-cream vendor. Though ice-cream had existed for a long time it was only the relatively recent introduction of industrial-scale refrigeration which made ice-cream production commercially viable. Italy was first into the field, and as a result Italian immigrants dominated the ice–cream trade everywhere.

Did you know?

The oldest pub in the city is the Old Queen's Head situated next to Sheffield Interchange, which is said to be the oldest domestic building in the city, dating back to 1475.

AROUND THE STREETS
OF SHEFFIELD

Pinstone Street Sheffield, pictured here in three scenes captured in the second decade of the 20th century, looks as quiet and peaceful as could be. The busy street connects the Moor and Fargate. At one end is the distinctive dome of St Paul's Church, now demolished. Originally built on the outskirts of the town, on land bounded by Pinson Lane (later Pinstone Street) and Alsop Fields (later to become Norfolk Street), the site itself was known then as Shaw's Close or Oxley Croft. The building of St Paul's Church was funded by public subscriptions in 1720 and 1721, with the first stone being laid on 28 May 1720. The dome was added in 1769. A Mr Platts of Rotherham was the architect. The other prominent building in the street is Sheffield's fourth Town Hall. It was designed by the London-based architect E. W. Mountford and constructed over a seven-year period from 1890 to 1897, opening on 21 May, 1897. A

over the British Empire are digging trenches and daily laying down their lives in what would become known as 'The war to end wars'.

Below: Here's Barber Road Sheffield in a photo thought to date from the late 1940s when Sheffield's trams were still plying their route along the street. Many people still living will recall this typical street scene with great clarity: not just the trams, but also the cobbled road, gas lights and the complete absence of television aerials and satellite dishes on the rooftops. How times have changed – and not just the outward appearance: indoors was a world away from today's easy

...ater extension designed by F. E. P. Edwards was completed ...n 1923. The design echoed to a certain extent the ...architecture of the adjacent St Paul's Church. The exterior is ...ouilt of 'Stoke' stone from the Stoke Hall Quarry in ...Grindleford, Derbyshire, and is decorated with carvings by F. ...W. Pomeroy. Over in France men from Sheffield and from all

lives - coal fires, no central heating, and 'wireless' meant the radio not an internet connection. Making a phone call meant nipping to the phone box, not picking up a 'mobile'. Anyone buying one of these houses would have had to pay a few hundreds of pounds to join the property owning classes.

H ere is a selection of photographs focusing on Fargate and the Town Hall Square area of the city. The splendid Victorian Yorkshire Penny Bank, seen to the right in three of these images, was built in 1888-89. The Temperance movement was in full swing by the mid 1800s and sharing this massive building with the bank was the Albany Hotel, an alcohol-free establishment. Adjoining the bank is Carmel House, which became the premises of the YMCA.

In the Victorian era, Joseph Woolhouse said in his "A Description of the Town of Sheffield", written in 1832 while cholera was raging in Sheffield: "In going up Fargate there was houses built on both sides. The Lords House stood a little on the North side of the present Norfolk Row. A very elegant old House, it was inclosed by a Wall in a half Circle and Palisaded. The present Duke of Norfolk was born in this house. This I expect is the reason why it was called the Lord's house, he being Lord of the Manor".

The view across Town Hall Square has changed dramatically over the years. The small group of mothers who stood in the middle of the square with their children, would 60 years later, be standing in the middle of Goodwin Fountain. Pictured right, is the picturesque central fountain, with its 89 individual water jets, which it is dedicated to the late Sir Stuart and Lady Goodwin. Sir Stuart was the founder of an important Sheffield steel and toolmaking firm. One of the donations was for the construction of a new fountain at the head of Fargate in 1961. The fountain was originally intended as a tribute to Alderman James Sterland from the Goodwins. However, it became known as the Goodwin Fountain and was eventually dedicated to them.

In 1998 the old fountain had worn out and was replaced by the new fountain in the Peace Gardens. Today, Fargate, pedestrianised in 1973, is one of Sheffield's most popular walkways. The shopping area has been endowed with a continental look and feel. With the traditional cobbled streets and the sight of the Cathedral at the bottom of the avenue. In the centre background of the picture above, is the Sheffield Telegraph and Star's clock tower, which is still a landmark today.

Did you know?
Sheffield was granted a city charter in 1893.

High Street has existed for as long as Sheffield has been a settlement of any importance. The first documented mention was in the 12th century when it was written that Worksop Priory owned five principal properties on the north side of High Street. Kemsley House designed by Gibbs, Flockton & Teather is a grade two listed building better known as the Star and Telegraph building. It was opened on the north side of High Street in 1913 and is named after Gomer Berry, 1st Viscount Kemsley, the newspaper proprietor. It now houses the headquarters of the Sheffield Star newspaper. Its white brickwork and elegant clock tower it is a familiar landmark and can be seen in a number of these photographs.

High Street suffered badly as a result of the Sheffield Blitz in December 1940 when many of the high Victorian buildings on the south side of the street were devastated by Germany bombing. These were the newer buildings which appeared as a result of the road widening at the end of the 19th century. All of the older shops on the northern side were spared by the bombing. Buildings which were destroyed in the Blitz included the Marples Hotel, on the corner with Fitzalan Square. Post war rebuilding of the damaged High Street was slow, it was not until 1951 that the damaged Walsh's store was demolished with a new store opening on 13 May, 1953. A new Marples Hotel opened in 1959 while C&A also rebuilt their store, although the building is now occupied by Primark. The early 1960s saw a radical change to High Street's junction with Angel Street when a decision was taken to give cars easier access to the city centre. This involved the creation of Arundel Gate, a dual carriageway which approached from the south and met the High Street / Angel Street junction at a roundabout.

Top right is an interesting view looking from the junction of High Street and Angel Street, towards Commercial Street in the distance. In this 1935 photograph the prominent building in the centre background is the former Gas Company offices at Bryward House. It was originally known as Panache House and this is carved above the western doorway of the building, today it is better known to readers, as Canada House. The Grade II listed building dates from 1874. To the right of the street are shops which include, G A Dunn & Co, Hatters, and the King's Head Hotel, at No1 Change Alley. Readers may remember that Change Alley was a short street that ran between Norfolk Street and High Street. It disappeared when Arundel Gate was connected to High Street. Roughly-speaking, the hotel backed onto the buildings that form the top-side of Fitzalan Square and was destroyed in the Sheffield Blitz.

To the left of the picture is C & A Mode Ltd and Montague Burton's on the corner. An immigrant from Lithuania at the turn of the century, Montague Burton developed a small men's outfitting business in Chesterfield and then Sheffield. By 1913 he

had five men's tailor shops, and for a brief period the headquarters in Sheffield. He also opted to live in the city and set up home in Violet Bank Road, Nether Edge, after his marriage in 1909. The business went on to become world's largest wholesale bespoke tailoring service. Every Montague Burton shop was easily recognisable, as they all had the same window dressing and in the name of the firm uniformly presented in bronze lettering on the marble.

There are a number of explanations as to how the phrase 'the full monty' (as in the 1997 film of the same name), originated. The most often-repeated derivation is from the tailoring business of Sir Montague Burton. A complete three-piece suit, i.e. one with a waistcoat, would be the Full Monty. There is plausible hearsay evidence from staff that worked in Burton's shops who confirm that customers were familiar with the term and often asked for 'the full monty' by name.

The scene played out in front of the Telegraph and Star offices would not be possible today, as High Street is part of the main Supertram route through Sheffield and vehicle cannot travel down the left hand side of the road. There is certainly no chance of seeing any vehicle parked or left unattended along the highway. The sight of

a policeman in a full length white coat, perched on a dias, is of a different age. As we can see in the earlier photographs the thoroughfares were built to allow horse and carts and the occasional stagecoach to pass through and eventually could not cope with the increase in volume of road users. At the time of this photograph, however, this was a common sight as for perhaps the first real time in our history, traffic flow in our city centres became a live problem. Traffic lights and roundabouts, largely instituted in the 1930s, eased the problem for a while, but many crossroads and intersections needed assistance from the long arm of the law as everything ground to a halt.

This view of Fitzalan Square (right) from 1964 is dominated by the statue of King Edward VII which is directly in the centre of this photograph. The bronze, granite and ashlar statue by Alfred Drury, is of King Edward standing on a stone plinth in ceremonial dress. After the death of Queen Victoria in 1901, the new monarch was considerably more visible than the reclusive widow queen. He threw himself into his new role with energy and his reign restored sparkle to a monarchy that been rather gloomy since his father's death 40 years earlier. He made a number of visits to Sheffield and was a popular

Fitzalan Square lies at the eastern end of Sheffield's High Street, about a quarter of a mile south of the Lady's Bridge bow of the River Don. This part of the city has been the market quarter since medieval times, and was once known as the Bullstake. The modern square took its name from the market hall that stood there in the Regency period. Fitzalan Square was created in 1881 when Market Street and its buildings were demolished; the early square had a substantial cab stand and clock. However, this was demolished in 1913 to make way for a bronze statue of King Edward VII by Alfred Drury (1857–1944).

Grade II listed White Building. Built in 1908 by Gibbs and Flockton, it is faced in faience, which was intended to resist the soot that blackened many of Sheffield's buildings at the time.

The early square also had the Electra Palace Cinema, which opened in February 1911. It became the News Theatre in 1945 and the Classic Cinema in 1962. In this picture from the 1950s, the News Theatre sits cosily between Barclay's Bank on one side, and the Bell Hotel on the other side. Part of the Cannon Group, the building had closed in 1982 with the final film for the audience to see was 'Rocky III. The building was destroyed by a fire in 1984 . The burnt out building (pictured below) was later demolished. The site is now occupied by an amusement arcade. Next door to the cinema was the Bell Hotel public house. Another public house, the Elephant Inn, stood on the corner where Norfolk Street entered the square. However, because of recent history, the best-known and most talked about structure in Fitzalan Square is the "Marples" building.

figure, recognised for using his common touch, dignity and enormous charm to bring the monarchy into the twentieth century. But as both King and as Prince of Wales, he was affectionately known to his people as Bertie, the playboy prince. The Edwardian era, which covered Edward's reign and was named after him, coincided with the start of a new century and heralded significant changes in technology and society, including powered flight and the rise of socialism.

A scheme to commemorate the late King appeared in February 1911 in the Sheffield Daily Telegraph, proposed by a prominent local citizen. This consisted of two parts, the monument and a "crippled children's home". Fitzalan Square was created on the site of the former Fitzalan Market, an area known as 'The Shambles'. The bulk of the funds were raised from local businesses and prominent citizens. The monument was unveiled by the Duke of Norfolk on 27 October, 1913.

Directly behind the statue is the General Post Office building Sheffield's Head Post Office operated in the square for almost ninety years. Built in 1910 as an addition to the 1897 post office building on Flat Street, it closed in 1999, with the main post office moving to new premises within the Co-op store on Angel Street. On the west side of the square is the

existence since 1657. By the 1850s the Angel was a family-run business and was officially being termed a hotel, which at its peak contained 55 bedrooms. It was a notable coaching inn before becoming a temperance house in the early 1900s. In its final days the Angel was the headquarters of Sheffield's special constables before it was destroyed in one of the German bombing raids in World War II. After the war the site was derelict for many years before it became the site of the ABC Cinema in 1961.

hese photographs taken of Angel Street in the first part of the last century, are far more interesting than any pictures you may see of the street today. The street takes its name from the Angel Inn, one of Sheffield's foremost public houses. Situated on the corner of Angel Street and Bank Street, The Angel, is thought to have been in

Visible in a number of these pictures is Cockaynes store, well known to Sheffield shoppers. In 1829 Thomas Bagshawe Cockayne and William Cockayne, the sons of William Cockayne, flax dresser, opened a draper's shop at 1 Angel St. The company was incorporated in 1899 by which time it had expanded into a large department store with its own cabinet making factory. This store was destroyed together with many of

the company's records in the Sheffield Blitz of December 1940. The company continued to trade, utilizing various premises in the centre of Sheffield, and were able to reopen the first phase of the new store on the old site in 1949. The final phase of rebuilding was completed in 1955. In 1972 T.B. and W. Cockaynes Ltd was taken over by Schofields (Leeds) Ltd and the name of the store changed to Schofields. The store closed in November 1982

A fantastic set of four photographs highlighting the changing outlook across Town Hall Square. In the oldest picture we can get a feel of Victorian life as we get a look at a rare view of the Jubilee Monolith erected in 1887. This was the year of Queen Victoria's Golden Jubilee and part of a national celebration of her 50th year as Queen. It remained in situ until 1905, when it was replaced by the Queen Victoria Monument which can be seen in the second image on this page. This Statue was created by Alfred Turner and was commissioned by Public Subscription. It was unveiled by Princess Beatrice (Princess Henry of Battenberg) on 11 May 1905. On the monument, the Queen is attended by two bronze figures representing Maternity and Labour seated on either side of the main plinth. The front bears the following inscription: "ERECTED BY CITIZENS OF SHEFFIELD IN MEMORY OF A GREAT QUEEN MDCCCCIV". Both monuments were removed and sited in Endcliffe Park.

Looking behind the statue of Queen Victoria we can see the building that we all recognise as the Wilson Peck warehouse, which at this time was the working premises for Johnson and Appleyard Ltd, cabinet makers.

> ## Did you know?
> *Sheffield has the highest ratio of trees to people of any city in Europe. 2.5 million trees.*

By the 1930s, horse-drawn vehicles had all but disappeared from city streets… the motor car was now king. This, however, presented an increasingly hazardous situation. In 1934 the highest ever numbers of road casualties - 7,343 deaths and 231,603 injuries - were recorded (this compares with 2,538 deaths and 228,367 injuries in 2008). Half the deaths were of pedestrians in built-up areas and this would not be a surprise when you look at this photograph and see pedestrians standing in the middle of a busy road junction. The fact that car-ownership was no longer the preserve of the wealthy brought a fresh dimension to the debate about safety. A new Road Traffic Act in 1934, reintroduced the speed limit, setting it at 30mph in built-up areas. It is certainly a busy scene and this may be to do with the fact that a celebration was about to take place.

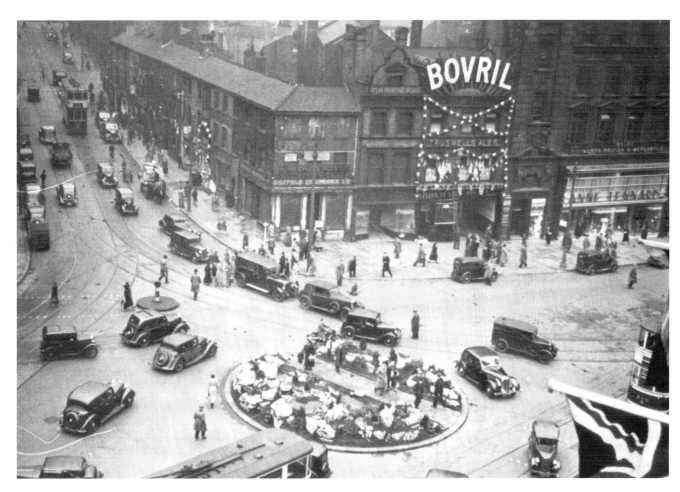

There is some evidence with the decorations above the Fleur de Lis public house and the Union Jack in the bottom corner, that this was May 1937 around the time of George VI's coronation. The street to the left is Leopold Street, looking towards Church Street, with the Three Tuns public house part way up on the right. Many of our readers may remember calling for a few in the Three Tuns and the Stone House before going to the City Hall dances.

In the most recent photograph we can see the outlook has changed yet again. The three buildings on the corner of Leopold Street and Fargate have new proprietors and the rockery has been replaced by the Goodwin Fountain. The fountain, with its 89 individual water jets, is dedicated to the late Sir Stuart and Lady Goodwin, and was constructed at the head of Fargate in 1961. Fargate extended to Pool Square until the 1960s, when it became part of Barker's Pool.

This is a very interesting elevated view looking across Town Hall Square, in the direction of Leopold Street and Fargate, possibly taken from within the Town Hall building on Pinstone Street. Many of the businesses in view will be well known to Sheffielders reading this book. Wilson Peck is arguably the most recognisable, having traded in the city for over 120 years. It could lay claim to being the longest running music and record store in the city. Across the road in the very clean looking white building, is H L Brown & Sons jeweler's with Cantors home furnishing and Dean &

Dawson travel agents next door. Today these buildings have been replaced by a more modern façade and Brown's have actually switched across to trade from the old Wilson Peck building. To the right of the picture is Bank Chambers and Anne Lennard costumiers. The area in front of these shops is mainly paved today and you would be highly unlikely to see a policeman on traffic duty like the one we can see in this photograph from 1952. Judging by the number of people crossing Leopold Street the cars and their drivers may have to wait some time.

The two photographs on this page are looking along Fargate from Town Hall Square. Both scenes are very similar with trams and motor vehicles in the foreground and the easily identifiable landmark of the Sheffield Star building in the distance. The photographer is standing in front of Winchester House and very near to the eventual flagship-shop of Arthur Davy and Sons Limited, which was in a purpose-built Tudor style building, at 38-40 Fargate. Davy's started up, in Castle Street, during the later 1860s. When the Fargate shop opened in 1883, it had food production facilities as well as a slaughterhouse. The building became known to Sheffielders as Davy's Building, (more recently to become a branch of W H Smith's), which housed the Victoria Cafe as well as the shop. The four carved animals' heads on the facade, still evident, refer to the butchery aspect of the business; the firm manufactured meat products, such as sausages and pork pies, in premises on Paternoster Row. When built the Fargate shop was described at the time as the largest provision merchant's shop in Britain.

wanted, then Davy's was the place to shop. Next door is the aptly named Weaver to Wearer, gents outfitters and just further along is, Davy's Mikado Cafe. We can still see the tramlines on the road, however the trams had disappeared from the streets of Sheffield the previous year. Some cities dug up the tramlines for scrap value when the motor buses arrived, whilst Sheffield chose to cover theirs up with tarmac. The old rails still come to light from time to time, when roadworks unearth them. In the background a tower crane reaches skywards, next to the GPO building in Fitzalan Square.

Above: Things are not looking too good for these two chaps on a motorbike and sidecar heading along the A61, London Road in October 1949. It appears that they are travelling headlong into the tram, but maybe they are actually following it, looking for a way to pass the stationary vehicle. They look a most unlikely pair of windows cleaners with their ladders and bucket perched on top of the sidecar. The Davy & Sons delivery van is obviously impeding the traffic somewhat, as he drops off or collects from one of their shops on the roadside. It is interesting to remember back to a time when businesses like Davy's and Gallons Ltd, were a common site around Sheffield. Small grocery chains and independant butchers shops were the norm at this time, and the traditional way to shop. Customers would be happy to wait in a queue to be served, while the shopkeeper weighed out the butter and tea and sliced the fresh bacon on his machine on the counter. Sadly, most of these businesses have now gone, together with the personal service we once took for granted.

Right: A fabulously busy and vibrant shot from the Haymarket around 1961. A similar view today would be dull and lifeless by comparison. The policeman on traffic duty keeps the oncoming buses waiting, as the large crowds cross the road in front of Davy's hugely popular food store on the corner of Castle Street. If it was a pie, cornish pasty or legendary tomato sausage that you

The 1847 Parliament Act led to the creation of Castlefolds Markets, on land between the Corn Exchange and the Norfolk Market Hall. It provided a covered letting space for the wholesale trade in fruit and vegetables. The Sheaf Open Market was also established on the adjacent site. This came to be known locally as "the Rag and Tag market" and became a popular place for Sheffielders to pick up a bargain. Perhaps the best description of the Sheaf Market is from a 1929 handbook which described it as follows: "The Sheaf Market is rather unique in its character,

crockery sellers on the two market days. In Spring the market is crowded with plants and flowers, which find a ready sale amongst the suburban residents and allotment gardeners. The Rag and Tag Market was a great source of anecdotes concerning market life in Sheffield. John Coates, a former trader, recalled the trader who sold miniature candlesticks made from gold, reportedly given him by an Afghan chief whose life he had saved in the Khyber Pass area. It appears to have been untrue.

In the photograph top left, facing page, shoppers and outdoor displays bring the old Sheaf Market to life and give an indication of the popularity of the old open air market. Pet baskets and other goods hanging from the outer wall, attract pet lovers to Ogley's super walk-round pet store and next door Aquarium. We can estimate the date to be 1964, as we are able to see that the Park Hill flats are already under construction on the skyline.

being a very large open market, and is chiefly used on Tuesdays and Saturdays by traders who bring their goods to market and offer them for sale on the stalls. Traders dealing in all classes of commodities attend, and the section used by the local fruit and vegetable growers, which is an early morning market, is let to

Below: A rather sad picture of Tudor House, better known to most as Newton House, on a rainy day in 1968. The former Victorian splendour and flamboyant architecture are less evident in this picture, although the ornate building still has its showy domes and lavish style. It was part of Sheffield's history as the first iron framed building in the city, when constructed in 1893.

Above: This is a view from what used to be the Moorhead area of Sheffield looking towards Pinstone Street and St. Paul's Church. Behind the oncoming tram, to the right, is the Nelson Hotel. When the Council developed the 'Civic Circle', this part of Furnival gate was completely reconstructed. The present building replaced the old Nelson in 1963. Sadly, the interesting archetecture was swept away to create space for the modern building, which was typical of the 'square block' style which was favoured by architects of the time. The Nelson was a popular pub until the late 1960s, when a murder was committed downstairs on the premises. In the 1970s, the pub was renamed the Hind and this remained the same until 1997 when it became an irish themed bar, Séamus O'Donnell's. Today, the present building on the corner of Union Street has been re-opened as the Nelson Rock Bar.

Many readers will remember shopping at the former Newton Chambers Showrooms, or just prior to this photo, P.W. Lacey Ltd, footwear and outfitters. There is an air of desolation about this view of Union Street, as it was the start redevelopment around Furnival Street. Work had already begun with the demolition of the Sheffield Picture Palace. Attention had turned to the old showrooms which were about to be developed by the Boden Group as a store and office. In more recent times the site was occupied by Currys and Union Street is a no-through road.

Above: An elevated view from the bottom of Dixon Lane (Shude Hill junction) looking down Broad Street towards Hyde Park Flats on the skyline and where the Park Square roundabout stands now. Immediately to the right is the Norfolk Arms and further along the 'Rag & Tag' market and we can just make out the Newmarket Inn on the Sheaf Street crossing. The Sheaf Market had been built to replace the 'Rag and Tag' market that had ajoined Castle Market. The Sheaf Market closed in 1973. This panoramic view is almost non-existent today, as the vista has been obscured by dozens of new flats.

Below, bottom and right: This rather forlorn looking building in the foreground is The Durham Ox, situated at 15 Cricket Inn Road, at the junction of Broad Street Lane. This pub opened in 1862 and closed in 1993. At the time of this photograph in 1961, many of the surrounding houses and buildings had been demolished. Many pubs bear the name Durham Ox after the bull calf bred by Charles Colling at Ketton Hall in 1796. Originally christened "The Ketton Ox" it became a national celebrity as

"The Durham Ox", when in 1801 the gigantic animal was purchased by John Day of Harmston, near Lincoln. He took the beast on tour of the country in a specially constructed carriage pulled by 4 horses. It was on show in London for almost 12 months. The bull died 15 April, 1807.

Regulars of the 'Ox' will find it hard to believe this photograph was taken over fifty years ago. Behind the well known watering hole we can see the Royal Victoria Hotel, adjacent to the railway station. In the distance, construction work is being carried out on the Pye Bank Flats. Their reign on the Sheffield skyline was fairly shortlived however, as they were demolished around thirty years after this picture was taken.

Sheffield Canal Basin, now known as Victoria Quays, is at the head of the Sheffield and Tinsley Canal, close to Sheffield City Centre. The basin dates from 1814, when the canal opened to connect with the River Don Navigation, allowing canal boats to reach the heart of Sheffield for the first time. When it opened on 22 February 1819 a general holiday was called and crowds of spectators, reportedly 60,000, gathered to watch the first boats, a flotilla of 10 arrive from Tinsley. Within the flotilla was one barge of coal brought from Handsworth Colliery - the first cargo to travel the canal. The basin was a busy, thriving transhipment point for many years, but trade declined as more goods were moved by rail and later by road. By the 1970s, it had declined into a forlorn and unwelcoming state, with the warehouses becoming dilapidated. The whole area received a new lease of life in the 1990s, when the warehouses were restored and new buildings were added. The Sheaf works were turned into a pub, the derelict railway arches were converted into shop units and a marina was created on one side of the basin.

Did you know?

Roughly a third of Sheffield lies in the Peak District National Park - no other English city includes parts of a national park within its boundary.

Chinese community, with the southern half of the road, in this photograph, is part of the A61. In the left background of this 1963 picture, is the Locarno Ballroom. Originally the building opened as the Lansdowne Picture Palace in 1914, then closed following air raids on the night of 12 December 1940. In 1947, the building converted for use as a temporary Marks and Spencers store, transforming into a Locarno Ballroom in the 1950s. Readers will remember that most young people went to dances at least once a week, going to dances in local church halls as well as in established clubs. The Locarno Ballroom building on the corner of London Road and Boston Road will be has had a variety of different names: Tiffany's Nightclub, The Palais, The Music Factory, Club Generation & Bed Nightclub. Today,

Below: A busy traffic scene at the junction of London Road and Cemetery Road, looking from The Moor. The roundabout is no longer there, but the building housing Barclays Bank is still standing. London Road is home to a variety of pubs, shops, accommodation, a library and a former cinema and ballroom. The northern end of the street is the centre for a sizeable the outer facade of the local landmark has been restored and serves as the frontage of a Sainsbury's mini market. The remainder of the original building has now been mostly demolished as part of the redevelopment works to create new retail units on the ground floor and additional student residences behind.

Above: People walk casually across the High Street in front of the oncoming line of trams. The old car turns left into Haymarket, which would be a problem today, as the Haymarket road is one-way in the opposite direction. The name Haymarket dates from around 1830, when the then Duke of Norfolk made one of his families several unsuccessful attempts to establish a hay and corn market in the town. The old name of Haymarket was Bull Stake. Here, certainly a bull was tied and quite possibly the town bull may have for hire as a sire. It may also link to this being the place where bulls were sold.

In the earlier photograph the premises to the right hand side of Haymarket include, Yorkshire Penny Bank, Nos 12-14, F.W. Woolworth and Co. Ltd. and Norfolk Market Hall further along the street. The building on the corner to the left, was later to become a 'Fifty Shilling Tailor' outlet. Many readers may not remember the Norfolk Market Hall which was built by Henry Charles, 13th Duke of Norfolk on the site of the late Tontine Inn. Opened on Christmas Eve, 1851, it was constructed in a classic style. The west front was rebuilt 1904-5 with shops opening on to the Haymarket. The sides and ends of the market were divided into about fifty shops. Double ranges of stalls ran down the centre, so the market was divided into four avenues. The building was demolished 1959 and replaced by the building in the second photograph below in the early 1960s, which included Timpson Shoes and a new Woolworths store.

Apart from the Co-op name on the side of a building, you would find this scene unrecognisable today. The view is actually looking down Angel Street in 1962, with the ABC Cinema on the left and Brightside Carbrook Co-op on the right. The Corporation Leyland double-decker bus is on its way up the hill to High Street, en route to Eccleshill. Evidence of the city's tram network remain in the foreground, two years after closure.

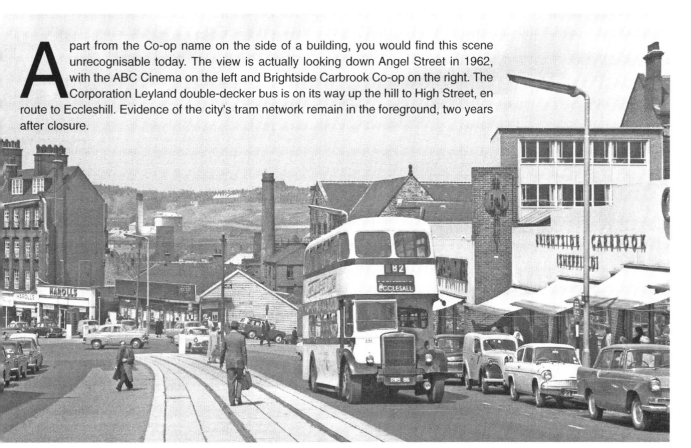

Below: A busy scene from 1965, looking from Market Place towards Angel Street, with High Street running across from left to right. This area was named Castle Square in the 1960s, to reflect the proximity of the square to the site of Sheffield Castle, which was formerly located a short distance to the north-west. Castle Square was originally known as the Market Place or the Shambles; markets were held on this site from 1296. A market cross was erected here in 1568 but was taken down in 1786, when the market moved into the new Fitzalan Market Hall that was built over part of the market square.

Many buildings in the vicinity of the Market Place were damaged or destroyed on the night of 12 December, 1940, when German aircraft bombed Sheffield. The bomb sites were cleared but most remained empty for many years. In 1968, many old streets were cleared to make way for the new Arundel Gate, a dual carriageway road that terminated at a large roundabout built on the former market place. Underneath the roundabout a network of underpasses and shops was built (with a central area open to the sky); this formed a complex that was officially designated Castle Square but became affectionately known locally as "Hole in t' Road". The road layout in this picture would look very different today as this is the site of Castle Square Station tram stop. In 1994, as part of the works for the construction of Sheffield's new Supertram network, the underground portion of the Hole in the Road was filled in. The roundabout was removed and the whole area landscaped.

ENTERTAINMENT LEISURE & PASTIMES

Right: In 1885 the Corporation bought 20 acres of land at Endcliffe Wood from the trustees of Robert Younge of Greystones, for £5,232. The intention was not only to provide public walks and pleasure grounds, but also to improve sanitation. Sewage from the newly-built housing north of the Porter Brook was flowing into the river from small tributary streams causing a serious health risk but acquiring the land enabled a sewer to be laid across the wood. In 1887, the Queen Victoria Jubilee Committee purchased an additional 9 acres of level land to the south-east for £5,045. When this photo was taken, a century ago rustic bridges and stepping stones crossed the stream which was stocked with trout. Seating, a refreshment room, and a lodge were also provided. The millpond at the east end of the wood was adapted for bathing. Walks were created alongside the dams, their outfalls turned into waterfalls.

Bottom left: A very cute scene from the 19th century, as two local Sheffield children sit and play with a tiny kitten. The kitten may be an unwilling player in the piece, as the kids possibly offer it some of their milk. It is thought that these are two boys whose family lived in the Owlerton Green area of Sheffield in the mid-1880s. It was not uncommon for boys from the Victorian era to appear feminine by today's standards. Boys traditionally wore dresses until about the age of 5 to make it easier to change their diapers. Most children during that time were not from wealthy, privileged families. It was common practice for them to wear clothes that had been purchased used and handed down. In those days, changing from dresses to regular men's clothing was significant as it showed that the boys were ready to become men. Until recent decades parents were not as concerned with declaring a child's sex.

Below: A fine array of vintage cars and their owners outside the Ashopton Inn, Derwent, in June 1904. This scene could not be recreated today, as the village of Ashopton is now completely submerged and covered in silt, beneath the waters of the Ladybower reservoir. The Ashopton Inn, a charming village pub and coaching inn has now disappeared following the flooding of the Derwent. Perhaps somewhat ironically, the Derwent Dams were to play a significant role in the Second World War, as the place where the 617 Dambusters Squadron of Lancaster Bombers, practised for their daring raids on Germany in 1943. In this photograph we can see members of the Sheffield and District Automobile Club standing proudly alongside their vehicles, ready to set off along the quiet lanes of the Derwent Valley.

Below: Firth Park was Sheffield's first publicly owned park, donated to the then town by steel manufacturer, Mark Firth. The opening ceremony took place on 16 August, 1875, when Mark Firth was Mayor of Sheffield. Edward, Prince of Wales, the future King Edward VII, and his wife Princess Alexandra opened it. The Clock Tower was the focal point of the park in its early days. It incorporated the park keeper's house, rooms for refreshment, and a verandah where visitors could shelter in bad weather. To the north was the ornamental lake which towards the end of the 19th century had not only about a dozen ducks of various breeds but also a pair of swans and a parading peacock. This photo from the 1920s is of a corner of the 'duck pond' and shows just what a popular spot this was to take the children on a summer afternoon.

Right: Forge Dam Park is the last of a string of attractive parks, which stretch along the Porter Valley from Endcliffe Park to open countryside. It is popular with families and is also passed through by the Sheffield Round Walk. A playground area has equipment suitable for children of all ages, including an impressive slide built into the hillside, swings and a tractor-shaped climbing frame. It has safety surfaces and is dog free. Walks beside the River Porter and through the woodland are popular. A cafe, with outdoor seating area, is also situated here. Sadly, what you won't find to day is this scene replicated. Ducks swim on the dam, but there are no longer wooden rowing boats. Down the decades the dam has been allowed to silt up and the rowing boats have long been taken out of the water. Some say it is ecologically better. Others miss the chance to just enjoy 'messing about in boats'.

Bottom right: The 19-acre site of the Botanical Gardens were designed and laid out in the mid 1830s by leading horticulturalist and landscape designer Robert Marnoc. Many of the design features which distinguish this style, such as winding paths, island beds and tree-planted mounds, can still be seen in the Gardens today. His work in Sheffield also includes the extension of Weston Park, High Hazels Park and the grounds of what is now the Kenwood Hotel in Nether Edge. Although designed by Marnock, The Gardens were established by a group of local residents who were concerned about the lack of public open space in Sheffield. They formed the Sheffield Botanical and Horticultural Society and purchased the land with £7,500 raised through shares. Over the years the

> ### *Did you know?*
> *Sheffield is reputed to contain over two million trees and is officially Europe's greenest city, a claim that was reinforced when it won the 2005 Entente Florale competition.*

fortunes of the Gardens waxed and waned. The Sheffield Town Trust became the owners in 1898, when entry to the Gardens became free. They managed the Gardens until 1951, when Sheffield Council took over for a peppercorn rent. Because so much of the original design of the Gardens is preserved, and because of the concentration of historical listed buildings, the Gardens are listed by English Heritage as a Grade II site of special historic and architectural interest.

This is an aerial view of the Hillsborough area from 1935. Running diagonally from bottom left to top right, is Penistone Road North. Sheffield Wednesday football ground is in the centre of shot with the River Don twisting around the stadium to the left, under the Leppings Lane Bridge. The stadium is sandwiched between Hillsborough Park to the south and terrace housing to the north. Football has been played at the ground since it was opened on 2 September 1899, when Wednesday moved from their original ground at Olive Grove. The first was, against Chesterfield. The match was kicked off by the Lord Mayor of Sheffield, William Clegg, himself a former Wednesday player. The stadium was known as Owlerton until becoming Hillsborough in 1914 following ground improvements. In this photograph the open end of the ground is the Spion Kop, named after a hill that was the scene of a famous battle in the Second Boer War. The stand remained open to the elements until a roof was added in 1986 after fans raised money to contribute to the cost. The scene is particularly quiet and this could be because residents from this part of the city were down in London, cheering on Wednesday in the final of the FA Cup. The Wembley final was a triumph for Wednesday as they won the game against West Bromwich Albion 4-2, with goals scored by Jack Palethorpe, Mark Hooper and Ellis Rimmer. Sheffield Wednesday Captain Ronnie Starling (below) carries the FA Cup down the steps from the royal box. The cup was presented by HRH Edward, Prince of Wales.

Sheffield Wednesday's 1935 Cup Winning team was; Sharp, Nibloe, Brown, Catlin, Millership, Burrows, Hooper, Surtees, Palethorpe, Starling and Rimmer.

Above: It is hard to imagine that regular gatherings like this ever took place. Apparently, however, this is a mixture of players from Sheffield United and some from Wednesday posing prior to their water polo match in the 1930s. This picture was taken at Hathersage Open Air Pool in Derbyshire. It is believed that the group includes: Third from left (front row), possibly Albert Cox, 1936-1952. Seventh from left (front row), Jock Dodds, 1934-1939. Ernest Jackson (on top diving board), 1933-1949. Goalie Jack Smith (also on top diving board). The group may also include Jock Dodds, Jimmy Dunne, 1926-1933, Jack Pickering, 1927-1948, and the Johnson brothers. Third from the back, seated, is Len Masserella, a pre and wartime Sheffield Wednesday winger.

Did you know?

Hallam F.C. still play at the world's oldest football ground, Sandygate Road in Crosspool.

Left: Seen here leading the side out at Wembley in Cup Final of 1925, is Sheffield United's Billy Gillespie, infront of 91,763 cheering fans. The 1924–25 FA Cup was the 50th season of the world's oldest football cup competition. Sheffield United went on to lift the cup for the fourth time, beating Cardiff City 1–0, with a goal from Fred Tunstall. During the first round proper on 10 January 1925, United had come up against amateur side Corinthians who were given a free entry to make the number of teams up to 64. True to form, United won easily 5-0. At the same time, near neighbours Wednesday, were making it a happy day for the city by beating Manchester United 2-0 at Hillsborough. Unfortunately for the Sheffield sides, they were drawn against each other in the next round three weeks later. United won a tight and exciting game 3-2 and went on to lift the trophy.

Sheffield United's 1925 FA Cup winning team that day was: Bill Cook, Charles Sutcliffe, Ernest Milton, Harry Pantling, George Green, Dave Mercer, Seth King, Fred Tunstall, Thomas Boyle, Harry Johnson, Billy Gillespie.

Left: 'William Comes to Town' was a 1948 British comedy film directed by Val Guest and starring William Graham and Garry Marsh. It was based on Richmal Crompton's 'Just William' series of books. The film was a loose sequel to the 1947 film 'Just William's Luck'. It was also known by the alternative title 'William Goes to the Circus'. The William books were a huge publishing success, and would be so for many decades, from the first book published in 1921, to the very last in 1970, the year after the author's death. The children from the Matinee Club are pictured here queuing up to see the latest William film are doing so outside the Stocksbridge Palace Cinema, in Manchester Road, Stocksbridge. The Palace, which cost £30,000 to build and had a seating capacity of 1,000, opened on 12, May, 1921. The cinema closed on 23 July, 1966, to become a bingo hall.

Bottom left: Whoever started the saying 'A bird in the hand…' could from the look of it have been a visitor to this local boozer in Sheffield. Regulars at the Burgoyne Hotel indulge in their two favourite pastimes, pigeon fancying and drinking. During the war the landlord Mr Harold Pantling and some of his regulars, all of them racing pigeon enthusiasts, turned their peacetime hobby into war work and bred birds for active service with the armed forces. To keep up interest after the war he had been holding regular 'Pigeon and Pints' nights. In this photograph from February 1946 we can see his customers in the bar's parlour, taking part in a competition for the best bird.

Below: The Old Queen's Head, No 40 Pond Hill, is thought to be the oldest surviving domestic building in Sheffield, and is the last remnant of the old timber-framed medieval town. It was built by the Talbot family in 1475, although the earliest known written record of it is in an inventory compiled in 1582 of the estate of George Talbot, the 6th Earl of Shrewsbury, and was originally known as the 'Hawle at the Poandes'. The building became a public house in 1851 and was named after Mary Queen of Scots who was imprisoned in Sheffield from 1570 to 1584.

The location was excellent for fishing and fowling as it was close to the River Sheaf and several ponds. These ponds, which formed in the area where the Porter Brook meets the River Sheaf, are now gone, but are commemorated in the local names Pond Street, Pond Hill (formerly Pond Well Hill) and Ponds Forge. Gentlemen would retire to the hall for refreshments after the day's fishing or hunting had finished. As it was situated on an important road leading to Lady's Bridge and the castle, it could also potentially have been used as a wash house or laundry for the castle.

The uprights on the face of the building have various figures carved into them including Spring Heeled Jack. He is a legendary figure thought to live in tunnels below the city, who would jump out to scare people. He was able to jump great distances and reportedly leapt over high walls.

This pub is reported to be the second most haunted pub in the country. It has seen many many changes to its layout and structure and has had its fare share of ghost sightings and reported paranormal activity. To this day the pub still has its ghosty visitors, but perhaps people have become more acustomed to them.

Above: Is this a junior version of Henry Hall taking charge of his first orchestra practice, in the late 1940s? Clearly the drum section is causing a problem to this budding band leader as he stands on a stool, with baton in hand. The children playing instruments in this percussion and piano rehearsal are from Denby Street Nursery School in the Highfield area of Sheffield, only a very short distance from Bramall Lane football ground. This was the age of austerity which Britain underwent immediately after winning the Second World War and this is reflected in the drab clothes the children are wearing. Many people expected rationing to be lifted as soon as peace was declared, but it was to be several years until the last ration book was issued. Denby Street Nursery was a local authority preschool establishment which opened in 1928 and demolished some 80 years later. In 2004 the school was amalgamated with Sharrow Nursery and Infants School on Sitwell Road.

Below: In this picture we can see a group of happy children enjoying a fun time in the playground at Thornseat Lodge, Mortimer Road, Bradfield, in 1952. Thornseat Lodge is on the borders of the Yorkshire Moors and was at this time a home for young children and toddlers. Originally it was built as a shooting lodge, in 1855, for William Jessop steel maker. It was converted into a children's home in the 1930s and remained as such for 50 years. After the war public attention focused on the plight of children without families. A national report on children 'deprived of a normal home life' was published in 1946, prompting a revolution in childcare. Known as the Curtis Report, it looked at the circumstances of nearly 125,000 children, including those removed from their families, children who were homeless or destitute, those orphaned by the war and children with disabilities. For the first time, children were acknowledged as the nation's responsibility. The home was vacated in the 1980s and although the building is now derelict, the evidence is still there; doors, a large washing machine and the outside swimming pool can still be seen on the site.

Left: This group of primary age boys, still segregated by gender for some activities, are seen in this photograph undergoing a physical training lesson at Wadsley Bridge Council School. The school was sited on the A61 Penistone Road North and was built in 1906. It was typical of the sort of educational establishment that catered for our youngsters after the Second World War. The school leaving age was raised to 15 in 1947 and many of these lads would have been unhappy at the prospect of spending an extra year at school. Those who did knuckle down however, had the chance to get to a grammar school via the 11 plus exam. This offered a pathway to an academic education and a route to college or university. Those who failed the exam went to secondary modern or technical schools, where the emphasis was on preparing for life as a member of the working classes. The school building was demolished in 1997 and is now the site of a large fitness centre.

The old Cinema House and Queen's Memorial flank this scene from the second decade of the 20th century. Opened in 1913, the Cinema House seated 800 and was one of the smaller city centre cinemas. The cinema, which boasted a tea room, had a narrow auditorium and patrons entered from the screen end of the building. Unhappily because of the width, its Cinemascope image size was severely restricted. Though the projection equipment was upgraded in 1961 that year would also mark the end of the road. On the evening of the Cinema House's final show in August 1961, all the Gaumont cinema's front of house lights went off. The cause was nothing more than coincidental, a blown fuse. The following day's Star however, always on the lookout for a story, got a quote from the Gaumont's (directly opposite) manager, Harry Murray, who said "engineers were baffled by the failure of the lights, but maybe it was just one old cinema's way of saying goodbye to another!"

Odeon, running for a total of 18 months between 1965 and 1967. In this view today you would see Mecca Bingo, which has operated from the premises since the cinema closed on 5 June, 1971. The last film to be shown was 'Carry on up the Khyber' prior to it be re-opened originally as a Top Rank Bingo Hall.

Below: The ABC occupied a city centre location on Snig Hill and was opened on 17 May, 1961, with Richard Todd in "Don't Bother to Knock". It was the most modern cinema of its day, fully equipped with a 60ft-wide screen (one of the largest in the UK). Built in a stadium style with a large stalls area and more steeply raked lounge area with more luxurious seats at the rear, the total seating capacity was 1,327. Stairs led up to a cafeteria area known as the Concourse, with large windows looking out onto Angel Street. We can get some idea of this from this photograph from 1963. The Concourse was converted into a 94-seat mini screen cinema which opened in September 1975. After being taken over by the Cannon Group in May 1986, the cinema

Above: The Odeon Theatre on Flat Street opened on 16 July, 1956, although unbelievably the original construction work is believed to have started some 17 years earlier. The Oscar Deutsch chain had planned to open the cinema in 1939, erecting the main steelwork, before war was declared and construction halted. After the war ended building work re-commenced under the guidance of architects Harry Weedon and Robert Bullivant. Seating was provided for 1,505 in the stalls and 814 in the deep balcony, which made it the largest post war cinema theatre to be built in England. In this photograph from 1964 we can see an old Morris Minor waiting at the Flat Street crossing in front of the Odeon. The people are heading towards the Grade II* listed old post office building, on the south side of Fitzalan Square. The Odeon was equipped to screen blockbuster films of the time, including "South Pacific" and "Cleopatra" which both had long runs here. "The Sound of Music" held the record for the longest screening at the

lasted only another two years before its closure and subsequent demolition. In the end, it was a relatively short lifespan of 27 years, for a cinema advertised as 'Britain's Most Modern Cinema'. After many years as a car park a Premier Inn Hotel now occupies the site.

exceeded only by the Regent and the Hippodrome. This picture of the Forum was taken in 1954. The Forum was opened on Saturday, 17 September, 1938, by the Right Hon. A.V. Alexander MP and featured a special screening of "One Night of Love" starring Grace Moore. As well as being a cinema, the building also had a stage. The first manager was Lawrence Cellini, a colourful character who introduced novel ideas. In the spring of 1941 Cellini's gimmick was 'Friday night is carrot nite', patrons being expected to make a

Above : The Tesco store on Herries Road was once the site of the Forum cinema. In its heyday the Forum was the largest cinema on any housing estate in Sheffield. Its capacity was charitable donation of a penny or more for a carrot, a few of which contained a surprise dividend. The Forum closed on 31 May, 1969; its last film was "Bullit" starring Steve McQueen.

Left and below: The photograph left is a night time Christmas view of the Regent Theatre in Barker's Pool, opposite the City Hall. The cinema actually opened on Boxing Day in 1927. As this was before the talkies came along, the early silent films were accompanied by a fabulous Wurlitzer organ. Designed by architect William Edward Trent, it could accommodate up to 2,300 cinemagoers. Built for cine-variety, it also had full stage facilities and a 150-seat cafe/restaurant. Taken over by Gaumont British Theatres in February 1929, it retained the name Regent until 27 July, 1946, when it was re-named Gaumont Theatre. The stage was still being used in the 1960s for one night concerts by artists such as Cliff Richard, Eddie Cochran, Bobby Darin, The Rolling Stones and The Beatles. It was twinned by Rank in 1969 and we can see a picture below left, from the opening. The gala event featured the films "Ice Station Zebra" and "Funny Girl" starring Barbara Strisand and Omar Sharif. The Gaumont closed on 7 November, 1985, with "Perfect", Madonna in "Desperately Seeking Susan" and "A View to a Kill". The building was demolished and shops, offices and a twin replacement Odeon Cinema was built on the site. The entrance to the new Odeon was on Burgess Street,

approximately where the stage of the Gaumont would have stood. The new twin Odeon opened in 1987 and closed seven years later.

This page: In these pictures we can see the Wicker Cinema, which was built before the First World War, but only opened as a cinema in 1920. The success of moving pictures was by no means guaranteed back then, so stage shows as well as films were put on by the management. In the event, people flocked to the modern miracle and were quite prepared to pay the high price of between 9p and 1/10d for a ticket. The success of the cinema continued to grow and by 1925 there were a reported 66 cinema halls listed as operating in the Sheffield area. By the time of the second photograph showing the renamed Studio 7, the numbers had dropped to below twenty. Although today we can count the number of cinema buildings in Sheffield on one hand, there is likely to be more screens in total than the highest recorded in 1925. Studio 7 closed for conversion to a triple screen theatre on 5 January, 1974. Studio 5,6 & 7 opened three months later showing mainly "X" rated films. It closed in December 1982, but despite a brief revival in 1986, it closed for the last time in 1987.

Did you know?

The Lyceum, Crucible and Studio Theatre make up the largest theatre complex outside London.

In the United Kingdom, at the time of these photographs, in November 1963, 'Beatlemania' was in full flow. "She Loves You" (released in August) had shot back to the number one position following blanket media coverage. This performance at the City Hall in Sheffield was part of the group's fourth nationwide tour of 1963. Such was the hysteria surrounding the Beatles that three girls in the audience fainted. One girl was so upset she was carried from the hall in tears. Following treatment for hysteria, by local St John Ambulance men, she was then allowed to return to the hall to watch the rest of the show. The Beatles rushed off the stage at the end of the show and, escorted by the police and still in their stage clothes, they piled out of a side door, into a waiting car and were off to a hotel in Doncaster. The Beatles made their Sheffield debut at the Azena Ballroom, in Gleadless, during a break in their tour with Helen Shapiro. They appeared there on 12 February, 1963. The promoter who had booked the group was the now famous Peter Stringfellow. Originally he had booked them to appear at St. Aiden's Church Hall, where he usually held his dances. However, due to the growing popularity of the Beatles, the police advised him to alter the venue and select larger premises, so he transferred the dance to the Azena.

Above: Though Teddy boys had their genesis in the 1950s, the increasingly insipid pop music of the early 1970s led to a remarkable resurgence of interest in early rock 'n' roll; and with it came the rebirth of the 'Ted' with his trademark drape jacket, bootlace tie and crepe-soled beetle crusher shoes. This photo of unidentified Sheffield Teds is from the mid-1970s. Though musical interest focused on early American stars such as Chuck Berry and Jerry Lee Lewis, the English rock 'n' roll scene flourished with such bands as the London-based Wild Angels. Early exponents of the reborn genre also included Showaddawaddy and Shakin' Stevens, although hardcore Teds tended to favour less commercial sounds, such as Yorkshire's Dave Lee Sound, Hotfoot Gale, Remember This, and Sheffield's Chuck Fowler Trio. The figure on the far right of this group looks very much like the late Dave Lee of the Dave Lee Sound.

Below: Rani, the 20-ton Indian elephant from Gerry Cottle's circus, was suffering from stomach ache, so circus manager Chris Barltrop asked the army if they could help. Ringmaster Martin Lacey said she had been eating less than half of her accustomed daily intake, which is usually 230 pounds of hay, cereal, apples and carrots. "She wasn't showing any other symptoms," said Lacey, "and the only thing I could think of was that she might have swallowed a discarded drinks can." As we can see in this very unusual photograph, Warrant Officer Philip Coombes, of the Army Corps of Royal Engineers, ran the mine detector across Rani's stomach, as the 16-year-old African elephant squatted on a circus stool with its front legs in the air. Coombes said that nothing metallic was detected. They concluded that Rani's problem was nothing more than indigestion, but the circus owners were happy with the extra publicity for its Sheffield show in October 1986.

Left: Fred Swallow ran his grocery shop on Talbot Road, until it was knocked down in September 1972. Prior to today's fast food and even faster lifestyle, shopkeepers like Fred provided a friendly, easy going and reliable service to the local residents. Customers had an undying loyalty for the man who could cater for all their grocery needs and wants. Younger readers may find it difficult to understand the importance of these stores to the local community. A closer look at the shelves behind Fred, give an indication as to the varied products available. Some may be familiar names but others like Trex vegetable oil, Needlers 'Maltonia Drops' and Parkinsons 'Blood and Stomach Pills, are rather less well known. Parkinsons' pills, manufactured in Burnley, were once known throughout the land – and even overseas. The company claimed that it sold more pills than any other business in the world. It was also the first anywhere to coat tablets with sugar to make them more palatable. Parkinsons' range of products also included Red Indian ointment. By the 1970s many small independent retailers were finding more turbulent. Inevitably with the increase in the number of cars on the road and a growth in the number of supermarkets, the fate of many corner shops was sealed.

Did you know?
Bassetts Liquorice Allsorts have been made in Sheffield for over 100 years.

Below: The summer of 1967 witnessed some gloriously hot days. And here is one of them. The scene is the paddling pools at Rivelin Park in Rivelin Valley Road. How many readers recall putting on their swimming cozzies and having a splash in the open air? There's something about children and water that must have been an irresistible combination since the dawn of time. The lido was used by thousands, and often referred to as 'Little Cleethorpes. The water for the blue painted paddling pools was taken directly from the adjacent river, and given a cursory filtering before being passed into the pools. Health and Safety fears about the water quality, together with vandalism and lack of maintenance would eventually lead to the pools being drained.

Right: Could this be classed as cutting edge fashion? In the foreground, June Hodgson can be seen striking a pose wearing a dress covered with razor blades, outside the Arts

Tower on Bolsover Road, in September 1967. The origin of the dress is not known but as this is part of a university it is probably safe to say this was a student-designed creation and very much of the time. The Arts Tower is visible from miles around. The building was officially opened by Queen Elizabeth, the Queen Mother in June 1966, has 20 storeys and at 78m tall it is now the second tallest building in the city, after the 101m, St Paul's Tower on Arundel Gate. It is also the tallest university building in the Britain. Designed by architects Gollins, Melvin, Ward & Partners, construction of the tower started in 1961 and lasted four years. A bridge at the mezzanine level links the tower to the university's main Library. The Arts Tower is used daily by around 2500 students and 300 staff and as its name suggests, the building originally housed all the University's arts departments, which had far fewer students in the 1960s. The Arts Tower and Library are Grade II* listed buildings. The paternoster lift within the building has 38 carriages that

could make it the largest of the few surviving in the UK. A paternoster is a lift made up of a chain of open carriages, each for two people that move in a loop up and down the building without stopping. The cars travel slowly enough so that passengers can step on or off at any floor they like.

Below: A joke is shared by a group meeting comedy legend Tommy Trinder, prior to the game between Sheffield Wednesday and Fulham on 2 October, 1971. Trinder, born in Streatham, South London, was one of the best-loved comedians in Britain during the period from the late 1930s until the 60s. A lifelong devoted supporter of Fulham Football Club, he was chairman of the club between 1959 and 1976. His catch phrases, 'You lucky people!' and 'If it's laughter you're after, Trinder's the name', combined with his trademarks; the trilby hat, the leering smile and the wagging finger, were almost universally recognised in Britain. He is seen here on the pitch side at Hillsborough getting a laugh from Lynne Unwin and her 19 male companions from Ashleigh Comprehensive School, in Sheffield. The final joke was on him, however, as the Owls won the game 4-0.

Cutting & Wear
Drilling Tools for the Oil Industry

The superior performance and quality of its products make Cutting & Wear the industry's first choice for hardfacing materials and systems, plus down hole tool development and manufacture.

Cutting & Wear was founded by Brian and Margaret Russell.

Frederic Brian Russell was born in Sheffield, in 1923. He was the son of entrepreneurial parents who in later life started their own cutlery business. He started his own working life in the laboratories at Edgar Allen's, a well known Sheffield steel company, where he met Margaret Bacon.

Margaret had moved to work in the steel works laboratories during the war to help the war effort.

At the start of the Second World War, Brian became a member of the Home Guard before joining the Fleet Air Arm. Training as a pilot took him to Canada, the Mediterranean, the Middle East and Australia. In 1945 he was part of the forces which took the Japanese surrender in Hong Kong.

Cutting & Wear Resistant Developments Ltd - 'Cutting & Wear' - Located at Smithy Wood, Ecclesfield, is an international, world-class organisation supplying 'down hole' tool technology to the Oil and Gas Drilling Industry across the World.

The company, established in 1968, was founded to serve the drilling industry with high quality products and services, based on leading-edge technology.

Leaving the Royal Navy as a Sub Lieutenant Pilot, in 1946, Brian married Margaret in August that same year.

Top left: (L-R) Jill Mcdonald, Margaret Russell, Brian Russell and Mark Russell. *Above:* Cutting & Wear Premises in Wincobank which they occupied from 1971-1976. *Left:* Machining stabilizers in the late 1980s.

Behind every great man there is a woman; in this case it was Margaret Russell. Without Margaret's encouragement Cutting & Wear would have never happened Margaret was always very proud how the company had developed.

Margaret was the daughter of the chief metallurgist at Steel Peech & Tozer, in Rotherham. He was also joint founder of the company's golf club, Phoenix Golf Club, at Brinsworth.

Before starting up the family business, Brian worked for Modern Hardmetals, on Holme Lane, Sheffield. It was part of the English Steel Corporation, and also owned an interest in a company manufacturing roller cone drilling bits for the oil industry in Manchester. Modern Hardmetals was set up to manufacture hard facing rods for this Manchester firm before it widened the product range into coal cutter picks, lathe tools and other tungsten carbide products.

Brian was a metallurgist and development engineer at Modern Hardmetals. There he pioneered vacuum furnace technology for sintering tungsten carbide and hot pressing tungsten carbide products too large to be sintered. He also worked developing new applications for the tungsten carbide, replacing high speed steels in applications such as slitting wheels for the tobacco industry and extrusion dies for the production of clay drainage pipes.

The first products manufactured by Cutting & Wear were tungsten carbide composite rod; the rods are still being manufactured today. 'AROCOY' was the trade name back then; today it is 'Supacutt'. Supercutt is crushed tungsten carbide in nickel bronze brazing alloy. It was an early example of recycling: the carbide was from used tungsten carbide inserts, either

from metal cutting, wood machining or forming tools depending on the application.

The newly developing North Sea Gas fields off the Norfolk coast presented the opportunity to establish Cutting & Wear. The drilling activity led to the establishment of a supply base at Great Yarmouth, which as well as loading the supplies for the drilling rigs also provided services to repair, maintain and occasionally manufacture the drilling tools. Cutting & Wear's composite rod was used to repair the blades of stabilizers which form part of the 'drill string' to keep the assembly drilling in the right direction.

Above: Queen's Award for Export Achievement presentation by the Lord Lieutenant, 1991. Below: Milling spiral drill collars on a converted lathe in the1990s.

electricity out-stripped the domestic supply.

The first C&W 'factory' was at the top of Bailey Lane at the end of a yard behind Morton's Cutlery Works where all Morton's grinding and polishing dust extraction systems were emptied. The workshop was only 30' by 15'. It was simply the end part of the knife-grinding workshop where two 'Grinding Troughs' had been filled in and concreted over - not very pleasant! However, it was cheap, and with no long term lease it was ideal for a fledgling business with very limited capital - Brian had sold his sailing boat to finance the business. A year later premises on Carver Street were rented in addition to the Bailey Lane workshop. This provided a base for research and development, a strong theme which continues to run through the company.

Brian manufactured and sold the products himself, with Margaret doing the accounts at home. Brian was, however, assisted from time to time by son Mark, and by casual labour and part-time retired men, not least Brian's father, Fred, after he retired in 1971. In 1973 came the employment of the first full-time member of staff. By 1975, Mark, who was then working in BSC's research and development laboratories, made the decision to join the company.

In 1971, came a move to a modern, but not new, factory, on an industrial estate at Wincobank. It overlooked the steel works in the Don Valley where clouds of red smoke would be emitted whenever oxygen-lancing was taking place. Of course such emissions would not be allowed these days! Margaret thought it was wonderful to watch the great Sheffield steel industry at work.

Jill Macdonald (then Russell), Brian's daughter, joined the company in 1977 after working at Walsh's (part of House of Fraser in Sheffield). Jill taking over the accounting and admin roles from her mother.

Brian and Mark concentrated on product development, production and technical sales. Jill was also company secretary, looking after sales, marketing and administration.

Peter Bacon, Margaret's brother, a director for many years, would also eventually join the company full-time between 1986 and 1992.

At the outset some products were manufactured in the garage at the Russell family home, but it wasn't long before the demand for

There were plenty of sparks at C&W too. On one occasion in the 1980s Vince, an ancillary, came in to the office with no particular urgency asking if someone would come out. Vince went away happy, but, he returned a few moments later a little more agitated to say a machine was on fire! Fortunately, it was only a few turnings on fire, although it was spectacular.

By 1976, Cutting & Wear required more space for the newly developing engineering products it was to supply to the oil and gas industry. After much searching, premises were found in Rotherham with vital yard space and a new industrial unit of 5,000 sq ft. There, led by Mark, the company began diversifying into engineering.

In the 1980s, Peter Bacon engineered a new type of directional drilling tool for a customer, a mechanically adjustable stabilizer. At the time revolutionary, manufacturing this tool moved Cutting & Wear's engineering skills to a higher level. Peter was also instrumental in gaining accreditation to BS 5750, which grew into ISO 9000.

Over the years the firm has managed to expand by taking on neighbouring premises to meet its needs. In 1981 the adjacent factory was taken over, which added a further 4,000 sq ft.

That same year C&W received an urgent call from a customer in Aberdeen; they wanted a tool grinding for a job in Doncaster!

An unusual place for our customers to be working, they were working on Britain's only on-land blowout. While drilling an exploration well, the rig had hit a high pressure gas zone and lost control of the well leading to the blow out. The find on Hatfield Moors, was later harnessed for industrial use and more recently was developed as an underground gas storage facility.

It was also the year that Keith Brown joined the company as a turner. He worked with the team until 2009 when he retired, Keith was taken ill and passed away shortly afterwards. Keith worked closely with Peter Bacon and Andy Ollershaw developing down hole tools. Keith saw the engineering side of the company evolve from manufacturing low tech stabilizer bodies to producing high precision directional drilling tools.

Joan Hoyland also joined C&W in 1981, and is still with the firm. Joan started as a fresh faced sub-contract cleaner and has since undertaken many roles from head gardener, to working in the hardfacing manufacturing shop. Joan was also responsible for the company's successful entry in the "Rotherham in Bloom" competition when they were winners.

Top, facing page: Mark and Jill at a Middle East Exhibition in the 1980s. **Bottom, facing page:** *Wally Howard and Juliet Cooper demonstrating Quick Tip at Offshore Europe, Aberdeen, in 1997.* **Above:** *Mark Russell visiting a customer in the Middle East looking at their stabilizer stock.*

Joan's role is one of House Keeper looking after the offices and sorting out lunches for everyone. She is a great ambassador for the company and never fails to make an impression on visitors. Joan is currently the longest serving employee and has 'seen it all' down the years!

In 1991, another adjacent building was taken with both overhead cranes and a further 6,000 sq ft. In 1998, a factory across the cul-de-sac was acquired and Cutting & Wear opened its Hard Facing Technology Centre.

That year the company was awarded the Queen's Award for Export. At the time the company was directly exporting over 80% of its output. A celebration was held at the Greasbrough Road premises which was attended by various dignitaries as well as by many company friends; an open day was held for employees and their families. Jill Macdonald, Juliet Cooper - sales, and Neil Simmonite - workshop manager, went to Buckingham Palace for the formal reception where they were presented to Her Majesty. The company has since also won two Smart Awards for technology.

Wally Howard was Sales Manager from 1993 to 1997. Wally had been a customer for many years, sending orders from wherever in the world he was working. When Wally joined the company he saw the commercial potential of an internal hardfacing process. This system was a novel way of applying tungsten carbide tile inserts onto oilfield stabilizers. This product was branded the 'QuickTip hardfacing system' and after successful application for patents the product was launched and has been an international success, now with around 50 licensees across the globe including the USA, Canada, South America, the UK, Europe, Africa, the UAE, Oman, Russia, Vietnam, Singapore, Japan and Australia. Wally, however, got itchy feet after a few years and moved back overseas, establishing repair shops and again ordering supplies from Cutting & Wear.

Andy Ollerenshaw joined Cutting & Wear in 1994 working in the drawing office and has been heavily involved in new product and tool development. Andy still works for the company, now as Technical Director. He has been involved in many projects including designing spiral milling systems, adjustable bends for drilling motors, Reamer tools and Hydrastab variable gauge stabilizer (Hydrastab was built for Toolbox which was part owned by Cutting & Wear and was sold in 2006 to NOV Varco, a multi-national oil service company.

Tony Mettam joined the company in 1997 as financial controller and was fundamental in helping steer the company through the lean times during the downturn in the early years of the 21st century. Working with the directors Tony guided the company through those troubled times. He was invited to be financial director. In 2007 Tony was runner up in the Yorkshire Financial Director of the Year awards.

In 2007, C&W aquired another 6,000 sq ft facility, and in 2009 took the building adjoining the Hard Facing Technology Centre, taking its total floorspace to 28,000 sq ft.

During 2010, C&W made the decision to build a new factory. It chose a three-acre site at Smithy Wood, half a mile from junction 35 on the M1 and convenient for visitors and for the majority of employees who had no further to travel and less traffic. All the staff moved with the company to the new 38,000 sq ft building complete with stockyard and further room to expand.

Company founders Brian and Margaret Russell both passed away in their eighties, having lived to see the small firm which began life in their garage become a business with an international reputation and some 70 employees.

Mark Russell is now Managing Director of the family firm; Jill retired from the company in 2003, but remains a director. Mark's son, Brett, joined the firm in 2005 and learnt the business from the ground up, starting in the hardfacing Technology Centre to his current role of Sales Manager.

Composite rod is still a major product, now sold under the trade names Supacutt and Supawear, the majority for metal cutting applications down hole. For wear resistant applications C&W markets Quick Tip. The majority of home sales are exported by UK customers. C&W itself directly exports worldwide to over 50 countries, and has licensees for its Quick Tip hard facing systems all over the globe.

C&W also supplies turn-key hard facing workshops for customers to manufacture and repair their own tools in any location around the world.

As complexity of oil and gas wells increases, so does the demand for drilling tools. Directional drilling tools are now able to steer themselves in 3 dimensions, analyse the formation they are drilling, and communicate to the surface with data in real time. The tools are manufactured from materials with higher strengths and corrosion resistance able to operate in

challenging environments. Cutting & Wear's highly skilled workforce use the latest manufacturing technology to machine these specialist drilling tools.

C&W's wide range of product for the industry is unique. Using its hard facing products in house, the company is able to continuously evolve products and applications to the benefit of customers.

The business plan is now to continue growing the company year on year, with the ultimate goal of establishing the world-leading standard for hardfacing products and equipment, and to champion UK exports across the globe.

Top, facing page: Joan Hoyland with her prize for the Rotherham In Bloom competition. ***Bottom, facing page:*** *Andy Ollerenshaw (left) and Keith Brown checking the operation of a hydraulic tool.* ***Above:*** *Cutting & Wear staff celebrating the company's 40th anniversary in 2008.* ***Below:*** *(L-R) Paul Jacobs, Stef Wasilewski, Bob Allen, Malcom Ellis and Mark Linley pictured alongside Junk Mills dressed with Supacutt composite rod.*

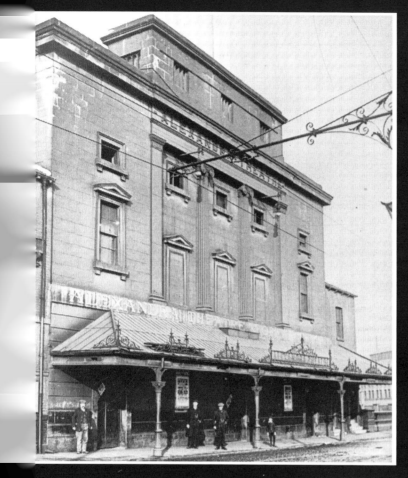

being provided for 61 in-patients. In 1868 the building was again enlarged and the number of beds increased to 105. The hospital was open to sick and lame persons of every nation, with separate wards for children. In 1890 it was decided to entirely rebuild the hospital. The first instalment, including the Out-patient Department and some new wards, was opened and the foundation stone of a Nurses' House laid, in 1895 by their Royal Highnesses the Duke and Duchess of York and as a result of which the name acquired its 'Royal' suffix. A dental department was opened in 1896. Closing in 1978, when it was replaced with the Hallamshire Hospital, the old building is now long gone.

Top right: The Grand Hotel in Leopold Street was completed in 1910 amidst great excitement and anticipation. It had long been held that Sheffield lacked sufficient first class accommodation to rival other large cities. The Hotel filled both a commercial and social void in Sheffield, and was to become both the place to stay and the place to entertain. The grand opening attracted huge crowds including many regional dignitaries. The hotel boasted over 300 luxurious bedrooms, a public lounge for taking tea and pre-theatre rendezvous, whilst the gold and crimson coloured ballroom and American bar ensured it was the place to be seen. Even the

Above: After the fire that destroyed the Surrey Theatre in 1865 Thomas Youdan went on to purchase the former Adelphi Theatre in Furnival Road and Blonk Street and reopen it as a music hall called the Alexandra Music Hall. The Adelphi began life as The Circus or the Adelphi Circus in 1837 and incorporated a ring for equestrian acts. The stage area was enlarged and it reopened as the Alexandra Theatre and Opera House on 12 October, 1865. It was reported in the press of the time that it could accommodate 3,000 to 4,000 people when it reopened. The Alexandra was in business for many years but finally closed on 28 March, 1914, and was subsequently demolished.

Right: Sheffield's original hospital was established in 1832 simply as a dispensary. In order to provide accommodation for in-patients, however, liberal subscriptions were given in 1857, 1858 and 1859, and the building was remodelled and enlarged, accommodation

Sheffield based barbers Taylor Taylor established a shop in the hotel for the use of both guests and style conscious public. The hotel also offered private self contained apartments for families, allowing local employers to accommodate whole families for extended periods. The Grand Hotel was the glamorous place to stay and socialise in Sheffield.

Below: Captured by the camerman in 1903, here's the Forge in Whitley Woods. The forge (now Forge Dam) was leased to

Henry Unwin & Co from 1838/39 to the mid-1860s and was owned by a Miss Silcock, a descendant of Thomas Boulsover who owned it previously. On her death it passed to her cousin John Hutton, who sold it in 1873 to a John Denton. Its proper name was Whiteley Wood Forge. There exists a plan of the site dated around 1826. There was also Whiteley Wood Rolling Mill later called the Wire Mill. In 1840-41 there were three wheels, an Emery Wheel, a Saw Wheel, and a Cutler Wheel; the first was to let in 1846, and after that is often listed as being 'empty' though the main works seem to have been occupied. The area was popular for walkers a hundred years ago and Forge Dam Park remains so today.

Did you know?

The Weston Park Weather station, established in 1882, is one of the longest running weather stations in Great Britain. The coldest temperature ever recorded in the city of Sheffield at Weston Park since records began, is -14.5 °C (5.9 °F), recorded in February 1895.

Right: The Old Town Hall was built in 1807–8 by Charles Watson, and was designed to house not only the Town Trustees but also the Petty and Quarter Sessions. The initial building was a five-bay structure fronting Castle Street, but it was extended in 1833 and again in 1866 by William Flockton of Sheffield and his partner for the project, Abbott. The most prominent feature was the new central clock tower over a new main entrance that reoriented the building to Waingate. At the same time, the building's courtrooms were linked by underground passages to the neighbouring Sheffield Police Offices. By the 1890s, the building had again become too small, and the current Sheffield Town Hall was built further south. The Old Town Hall was again extended in 1896-7, by the renamed Flockton, Gibbs & Flockton, and became Sheffield Crown Court and Sheffield High Court. In the 1990s, these courts moved to new premises.

Bottom left, facing page: Sheffield's Town Hall on Pinstone Street, was built considerably later than those of the same period in other industrial centres of Northern England. It was not until 1886 that the Council obtained the land on which the Town Hall now stands and the Council launched a competition for architects to design a Town Hall. A design by the London-based architect E. W. Mountford was judged the best and work to construct the Town Hall took place over a period between 1890 to 1897. The building was officially opened on 21 May, 1897 by Queen Victoria. The design echoed to a certain extent the architecture of the adjacent St. Paul's Church of 1720 (now demolished). The exterior is built of "Stoke" stone from the Stoke Hall Quarry in Grindleford, Derbyshire, and is decorated with carvings by F. W. Pomeroy. The friezes depict the industries of Sheffield, and the 64-metre-high clock-tower is surmounted by a statue of Vulcan. An extension, reportedly costing £115,600, was added in 1923. The opening of the extension was carried out by The Prince of Wales on 29 May of that year, twenty-six years after Queen Victoria had performed the original opening ceremony.

Below: Here's a busy picture showing Moorshead in the early years of the 20th century. The scene is now much changed — most notably by the removal of the Crimean war memorial. The inscription on the base read: "This monument in memory of those natives of Sheffield who fell in the war in the Crimea was erected by public subscription AD 1863." Between 1957 and 2004 the Crimean War Memorial was re-sited in the Botanical Gardens. The monument had been relocated to the Gardens from the city centre during redevelopment of the Moor shopping area. In 2004, it was dismantled and is now in store awaiting full restoration and re-location within Sheffield. Behind the monument can be seen one of 200 branches of the Public Benefit Boot Company. Founded in Hull in 1875, the firm aimed to supply poorer folk with footwear they could afford.

Above: Pictured here in the late 1920s is the Queen Victoria Monument in Town Hall Square. On the left is the Town Hall, and on the right Town Hall Chambers. The bronze figure of a crowned Queen Victoria holding an orb and sceptre stands atop a limestone plinth. The figure is about nine feet high. She is attended by two bronze figures representing Maternity and Labour seated on either side of the main plinth, each about six feet high. 'Maternity' is a young woman holding a baby with her left arm around a young girl. 'Labour' is a young man sitting on an anvil with a sledgehammer propped against his left knee. The base is signed: 'Alfred Turner SC. 1903'. The front

bears the inscription; 'Erected by citizens of Sheffield in memory of a great queen MDCCCCIV'. Unveiled by Princess Beatrice of Battenburg on 11 May, 1905, the monument was moved to Endcliffe Park in 1930.

Left and above: Firth Court stands at the heart of the University of Sheffield precinct. The building was opened by King Edward VII and Queen Alexandra in 1905, the same year that the University of Sheffield was granted its royal charter and officially came into being. Firth Hall is named after Sheffield steel manufacturer Mark Firth, who played a key role in the University's early development. The building originally housed the University's Arts, Science and Medicine departments. The University of Sheffield was originally formed by the merger of three colleges. The Sheffield School of Medicine was founded in 1828, followed in 1879 by the opening of Firth College by Mark Firth to teach arts and science subjects. Firth College then helped to fund the opening of the Sheffield Technical School in 1884 to teach applied science, the only major faculty the existing colleges did not cover. The three institutions merged in 1897 to form the University College of Sheffield.

Did you know?

Sheffield College ranks as one of the largest further education colleges in Europe.

Sheffield University has associations with five nobel prize winners since 1945. Notable British figures amongst their alumni include David Blunkett, Eddie Izzard, Jessica Ennis and pioneers Amy Johnson and Helen Sharman

The corner of Fitzalan Square that adjoins the High Street was first occupied by a hotel in about 1870. From 1886, the premises were owned by John Marples, who kept a licence under the title of the Market Street Wine Vaults. Even after a subsequent name-change to the London Mart, the establishment was familiarly known as 'Marples.' It was an imposing building, standing seven storeys high, with a concert hall, residential suites and a grand lounge as well as a number of bars and guestrooms.

On the night of Thursday, 12 December, 1940, German bombers attacked Sheffield in what has become known as the 'Sheffield Blitz'. Their target was the steel works producing armaments in the east end of the city; however, a mistake in navigation caused the city centre to become the main target. Fire bombs caused widespread panic, and many people took shelter in the Marples' extensive cellars, believing they were safe under the robust seven-storey building. At 11. 44 p.m. the Marples building took a direct hit from a bomb which plunged through the building and detonated just above the cellars, killing approximately 70 people and reducing the building to a 15-feet-high (4.6 m) pile of rubble. The next day seven men were dug out of the rubble still alive, as a small section of cellar roof had, amazingly, withstood the impact. More than a thousand tons of rubble was lifted from the corner of the square.

The Marples site stood derelict until 1959 (see picture bottom left) when the brewing company John Smiths opened a new public house on the site, this time officially called "The Marples". The pub closed in 2002 and the following year was occupied by the Hein Gericke motorcycle clothing and accessory outlet.

Left and below: A rare picture showing the demolition of St Paul's Church, on Pinstone Street. Founded in 1740, St. Paul's stood next to the Town Hall. Following slum clearance in the 1930s, the church's congregation slumped, and St Paul's closed. In 1938 the church was demolished to make way for an extension to the Town Hall. The organ was removed to All Saints, in Wingerworth, while the Chantrey memorial was moved to Sheffield Cathedral. Due to the outbreak of war in 1939 the Town Hall extensions were halted and the site was laid out as an open garden. Originally given the title of "St Paul's Garden", it later became known by the people of Sheffield as the "Peace Gardens".

Right: The Cutlers' Company was established by a parliamentary Act of Incorporation in 1624 and for almost four hundred years has sought to maintain the standards and quality of Sheffield manufactured cutlery and steel products and to promote the name of Sheffield. In 1638, shortly after it came into being, the Company bought land for their Hall on Church Street, Sheffield, opposite the parish church, which is now the Cathedral. The second Hall was built in 1727 and the present Hall, a Grade II* Listed building, was built in 1832, being extended in 1867 and 1888. Over the years, it has served as a focus for the Company's activities and as a venue for social events - both for the Cutlers' Company and for Hallamshire.

Below: This early aerial view illustrates perfectly the proximity of Cutlers' Hall to the Cathedral. In the bottom left corner we can see the Kemsley House and the High Street junction with Church Street and Fargate; the corner that was to become known locally as, 'Coles Corner'. The main picture to the right, gives a good indication of how the space in front of the Cathedral has changed to become a much more people friendly environment. The Cathedral Church of St Peter and St Paul, originally a parish church, was elevated to cathedral status when the diocese was created in 1914.

Below: A very busy but relaxed scene looking across Church Street towards Cutlers Hall from the Cathedral gardens, probably from the mid to late 1960s. The rare sunny conditions seem to have brought out the local people in force. Church Street was originally named Church Lane. In 1785 it was widened by taking a section of the nearby churchyard which resulted in the exhumation of several bodies and coffins. This produced adverse reaction from local inhabitants who directed their wrath against the vicar, the Reverend James Wilkinson. Church Street does not have any retail shops on it, but it does have some of the more significant buildings in Sheffield as Cathedral and the Cutlers' Hall both stand on Church Street. The Cathedral is a grade one listed building. Construction started in 1430 although a church has existed on the site since the twelfth century. The Cutlers Hall was built in 1832 and is the headquarters of the Company of Cutlers in Hallamshire. After 1994 this view would look very different, as Church Street now has its own Supertram stop, directly in front of the Cathedral and the traffic flow is one-way from left to right, off Leopold Street. The Austin commercial van in the centre of shot would in fact be facing the wrong way today.

In the large photograph we get a fabulous elevated view along Barker's Pool towards the Grade II* listed City Hall. One of the earliest known references to Barker's Pool comes from the records of the Burgery of Sheffield for 1570. The name may derive from a "Barker of Balme" mentioned in a deed dating from 1434. At this time the area was known as Balm Green and was on the edge of the town.

Terraced properties and shops along one side of the square were demolished around 1923 to make way for the construction of City Hall. The building was designed in 1920 by E. Vincent Harris, but construction was delayed eight years because of the economic climate in the early 1920s. Eventually work started with the laying of the foundation stone in 1929 and the City Hall was officially opened on 22 September, 1932. Since then, the City Hall has played host to some of the most famous names of the 20th century and it continues to be an exciting entertainment and arts venue. Many world-famous artists have also appeared there as well as providing a venue for many local and community events.

In the main picture we can also see Barker's Pool Gardens, also know as, Balm Gardens or City Hall Gardens. They werer opened on 3 August, 1937, as a gift to the city by J.G.Graves, with the intention of preventing any further development so as to preserve the setting of the City Hall. The main feature was an ornamental fountain (below) with 16 jets of water spraying onto a stainless steel globe. It was in the centre of an octagonal paved area with flower beds and grass plots. The lower area was a pool surrounded by a flower bed and a paved area. Next to this we can see the white building which is the Grand Hotel. We can date this picture to the early 1960s as in the foreground is the empty plot of land where Cinema House once stood. The building was sold to property developers in 1959 and this led to the final show on 12 August 1961, with John Wayne in "The Horse Soldiers" and Burt Lancaster in "The Devil's Disciple". The Cinema House was then demolished later in the year with a new development of offices and shops rising up on the site.

Did you know?

The shots inside the club for the Full Monty Show were filmed at the Shiregreen Working Men's Club, on Shiregreen Lane.

Park Hill estate dominates the skyline, as it towers above Sheffield Midland station. Built between 1957 and 1961, following the first post-war slum clearance, Park Hill was the most ambitious inner city housing development of its time. Designed by young architects, Jack Lynn and Ivor Smith, the concept of the flats was described as 'streets in the sky'.

Broad decks, wide enough for milk floats, had large numbers of front doors opening onto them. Each deck of the structure, has direct access to ground level at some point on the sloping site.

The site also allows the roofline to remain level despite the building varying between four and thirteen stories in height. To maintain the strong sense of community, neighbours were re-homed next door to each other, old street names were re-used (Gilbert Row, Long Henry Row, Norfolk Row) and cobbles from the terraced streets surrounded the flats and paved the pathways down the hill to Sheffield station and tramlines.

Despite its Brutalist style of architecture, the estate proved to be very popular and was fully occupied until the early 1980s, when it fell into decline due to lack of investment and social change. Even now, after receiving Grade II* listed status in 1998 (the largest listed building in Europe), inhabitants of Sheffield are split on the matter of Park Hill; many believe it to be a part of Sheffield's heritage, while others consider it nothing more than an eyesore and blot on the landscape.

The idea behind the Park Hill Estate was to replace slums with ultra-modern living, maintaining the sense of community but allowing residents modern facilities that they had never experienced. Parkhill was not alone; around the same era, two other locally well-known complexes were constructed in Sheffield. These were Kelvin Flats and Hyde Park Flats. Kelvin Flats has since been demolished, whilst Hyde Park was partially demolished and the remainder was redevolped to providee accommodation for the World Student Games in 1991.

This aerial photograph highlights even more the distinctive, snake like, shape of the Park Hill Flats. Amazingly it was taken over 40 years ago, but is still standing today. The three high-rise council blocks that were on Claywood Drive to the left of shot, did not make it however as they were demolished within the last ten years. The spike to the left of the flats, next to Clay Wood, is actually the Cholera Monument, a memorial to the 402 victims of a cholera epidemic of 1832. The buildings to the centre left of the image include the Sheffield Polytechnic, later to be granted University status, with the bus station directly in front.

WORLD WAR

Below: A rare picture of a tank on the streets of Sheffield during the First World War. There is nothing sinister in this photograph, as the tank was in the city to promote the sale of War Bonds in 'Tank Week'. War bonds are debt securities issued by a government for the purpose of financing military operations during times of war. They generate capital for the government and make civilians feel involved in their national militaries. The campaign extended to the whole of the country, the touring tanks would spend a week in a town or city, with two young ladies selling war bonds from a table set up inside the tank. A competitive spirit was engendered between the visited locations, the town or city that invested the most per capita would win the tank "Egbert". The six tanks on the country-wide tour were: 130 Nelson; 113 Julian; 119 Old Bill, 141 Egbert; 138 Iron Ration and 137 Drake. The tank would be accompanied by soldiers and artillery guns and would arrive with great fanfare, while civic dignitaries and local celebrities would be out in force.

The eventual winner of the competition was West Hartlepool who raised £31 9s 1d per capita, the equivalent to approximately £1300 today.

Right: This is a graphic picture of the wrecked Marples Hotel, after the Sheffield 'blitz' that struck during the night of 12 December, 1940. Even the rescue teams from the civil defence organisations were stunned by the carnage around Fitzalan Square. In their heart of hearts, they knew it was on the cards, but nothing prepared them for the stark reality of the total destruction. It is hard to imagine how seven men were rescued alive from the cellars beneath the hotel. Sheffield manufactured munitions, armour plate and aircraft parts for the military and was a strategic target for the enemy. People knew what was coming and rushed to take what shelter they could, but death and destruction were inevitable once the bombs started falling.

Precautions Act, which came into being on 1 January, 1938. While ARP wardens and firemen fought the fires, women in the WVS set up mobile canteens to keep them refreshed. By doing this, they placed themselves in the heart of danger with collapsing buildings a constant threat. Sheffield W.V.S. carved out for itself a special place in the city's war effort. Quickly into its stride hey opened a Hospital Supply Depot at 246, Fulwood Road, closely followed by a second at Tapton Court, where members made bandages, swabs, and hospital clothing in

Below: A WVS mobile canteen offers tea to people in the heavily bombed area around St Mary's Road. Working from a converted Rolls Royce the women volunteers provide much needed refreshments after the bombings of 12 December 1940. The ladies of the Women's Voluntary Services worked tirelessly throughout the war with a 'never say no' attitude. The WVS was established in 1938 by Stella Isaacs, the Dowager Marchioness of Reading. They were to act as a support unit for the ARP and the 'terms' of its work was set out in the Air Raid

large quantities throughout the war years. By the time the Luftwaffe attacked the city, 1,600 women were ready for this work. From January, 1941, a W.V.S. mobile canteen was at the service of members of the Forces stationed outside the city. By the end of the war it had travelled 50,000 miles, and provided thousands of teas. It helped in other ways, too, particularly in providing many personal necessities not easy to obtain in the remote areas. Apart from running the mobile canteens, these unpaid workers delivered water in tankers where the water supply had been damaged; ran knitting circles to knit socks for the soldiers; collected and distributed clothing and household items to those who had lost everything to bomb damage; helped to organise the housing of evacuees and much, much more.

Early in the new year of 1941, King George and Queen Elizabeth paid a visit to commiserate with those who had suffered the most during the Sheffield Blitz. She more than her shy and diffident husband, was the one with whom the people of Sheffield bonded. Even her body language in this photograph shows how warmly and sympathetically she listened to the stories of these homeless people. After Buckingham Palace was hit she said that she could now look London's east-enders in the face. She clearly was up for the fight and stayed to face Hitler along with the rest of us. No wonder she became a national treasure, known affectionately as the 'Queen Mum'.

Above: A scene of utter devastation from 1941 as a double decker bus is among many that got caught in the blast from a bomb during an air raid in Sheffield. Needless to say, the clear-up operation and emergency work that followed was huge. Over half of the city's 150,449 houses were damaged, with 2,906 destroyed or beyond repair. Half the city was left without electricity and many areas were without gas and water for some weeks.

Below: You can almost hear the cry; 'Eyes left!', as a unit of the York and Lancaster Home Guard Regiment (initially the LDV) salute Sir Ronald Adam, as they proudly march through Town Hall Square, in September 1940. As many readers may remember, military parades were to become an accepted part of life during the Second World War and a real morale booster. The sounds of the far-off beat of the drums, would bring the local residents scurrying out of their houses to watch the soldiers march by. These parades undoubtedly made the average person on the street, feel more in touch with the military. British television comedy Dad's Army (1968–1977), which followed the formation and running of a platoon in the fictional south coast town of" Walmington-on-Sea", and is widely regarded as having kept the efforts of the Home Guard in the public consciousness.

ife would never be the same again for the residents of Sheffield after a night of German bombing on 12 December, 1940. The next day a massive clear-up operation would have to begin, but for now everyone had to come to terms with the enormity of what had just happened. Deadly incendiaries and high explosive bombs, left behind a blazing inferno and hit huge areas of the city. In the main picture we can see the premises of John Walsh Ltd ablaze after the bombings. Mangled trams, twisted metal and shattered buildings everywhere only told part of the story. Sheffield firemen battled hour after hour to try and bring the fires under control but in some cases it was almost impossible. It often took days of hard work to make the smouldering premises completely safe. John Walsh Ltd was a family-owned store opened in 1875 in High Street. This shop was to grow into a large department store but was destroyed by the Sheffield Blitz and subsequently a temporary wartime store was opened at The Mount. By the end of 1941, the company also operated from its premises at 41-45 Fargate, which had previously been used as assistants' accommodation, and at Church Street. Acquired by Harrods in 1946, the store was rebuilt in 1953 and renamed and reopened as Walsh's.

masks. The government thought that younger children would be scared of the gas masks so they produced a specially designed mask which became known as a 'Micky Mouse' gas mask, which was brightly coloured in red and blue.

Right: During the war life changed for everybody, including children. For most, the war years were a time of anxiety. Children had to grow up quickly as many had to look after themselves and younger siblings while their mothers worked. Seen here in 1939, are two small boys in gas masks being guided by a warden. The boys look quite relaxed as they receive instruction, as every effort was made to accustom children to the frightening and claustrphobic gas masks, that made the wearers look like fearsome monsters. Because of the threat of mustard gas attacks, children in particular had regular half hour gas mask drills. The masks, when new, were very stiff and tight and

Above: Evacuation of Children from Britain's major cities began at the outbreak of the Second World War. Most were sent to the countryside in the hope that they would be safe from the expected bombs and gas attacks. The evacuation was arranged via the schools and whole classes, even whole schools, were evacuated together. Despite the difficult times and uncertainty, kindly nurses and assistants would always try and ensure that young children got a bath, whether they wanted one or not. The tin bath was filled and emptied using a white enamelled bucket with a blue rim and a wire and wooden handle. The water depth of a bath was regulated by the government at four inches (100mm). This was to save both gas and water. The soap was ordinary household soap. Children today are often greeted with the phrase; "You kids don't know you're born". Tin baths, outside loos with squares of newspaper hung on an old wire coat-hanger, rats in the backyard shed, bed bugs and a host of other verminous creatures were part of life in those days and hard to comprehend for the youngsters in this high-tec age.

Right: No-one liked wearing gas masks, but young mothers with babies had a particularly difficult time during the Second World War. Gas masks were issued to all British civilians at the start of the war as there was a very real fear in Britain that Nazi German bombers would drop poison gas bombs. Babies however, had special cradle-like respirators which would only be issued if an emergency situation arose. Babies were put inside the case and when all the covering flaps were folded and the straps closed up. The baby was totally enclosed and fresh air was pumped in, using a hand pump, through a filter on the side ensuring the infant inhaled no gas. Mothers were greatly affected by the thought of their babies suffocating inside the gas

worth remembering only two years earlier, health secretary Aneurin Bevan had opened Park Hospital in Manchester and this marked the birth of the NHS system and the climax of a hugely ambitious plan to bring good healthcare to all. For many of us, it is difficult to imagine life before the NHS, when healthcare was unreliable and treatment had to be paid for. During the war, children had their own ration books which entitled pre-school children to an allowance of cod-liver oil and orange juice. Long before the advent of the cod liver oil capsule, the recommended spoonful of cod liver oil was administered to the youngest children every day. Children might have screwed up their noses at the fishy taste, but the nourishing cod liver oil went a long way towards keeping them healthy. The vitamin-packed orange juice was far more palatable, and artful mothers would often use the orange juice as a bribe. Later it became available as 'cod liver oil and malt', a totally acceptable brown sticky substance that tasted like toffee and had to be spooned out of a large jar. It has been said that child nutrition in the 1950s was superior to today, according to researchers - despite the food shortages of the post war period. Modern children fare worse for intake of several key nutrients, including fibre, calcium, vitamins and iron. In fact, rather surprisingly, the 1950s diet was almost in line with current recommendations on healthy eating for children.

uncomfortable to wear. Some may have found these drills hard to take seriously, especially older children, when they discovered blowing air out through the rubber made 'rude' noises. Such was the fear of gas attacks during the Second World War, that by September 1938 approximately 38 million gas masks had been distributed. However, the populations' fear abated as the war progressed and the expected gas attacks never materialised.

Right: It was possibly the acute wartime shortages of food and supplies which made doctors, health workers and mothers alike very aware of the health of the new generation, and children were carefully weighed, measured and immunised against illness, as can be seen in this Child Welfare Clinic picture in 1950. It is

Below and right: When VE Day finally arrived the whole country erupted with a mixture of joy and relief. After nearly six years of fighting the Germans it was all over. The desperate days of the blitz were temporarily forgotten in a blaze of flags, fireworks and floodlights. As Martha and the Vandellas said, there was "Dancing in the Street" amidst parties which took place on virtually every street in the city. Trestle tables were dragged out of church halls and schoolrooms as neighbours mucked in together to set up impromptu parties. Celebrations can been seen in full swing in this photograph from one of the parties taking place in Hoyland Street, Wincobank, in May 1945. A full week's rations were used to provide sandwiches, buns, cakes and jugs of lemonade for the children. Dancing to records on an old gramophone, we had not partied like this since the Coronation in 1937.

Powerful childhood memories were forged by the parties which were organised in local communities across the country. This is quite a striking image when you consider that these children in Rushdale Avenue (right), are celebrating Victory in Europe by raising a Union Jack flag and preparing to burn an effigy of Hitler. VE Day was 8 May, 1945 and celebrations on a massive scale followed. There were street parties, fireworks and bonfires on which effigies of Hitler were burnt. Crowds gathered en-mass in the city centre and complete strangers hugged and kissed each other. The lights blazed and Winston Churchill addressed the nation. On the actual day trestle tables were set up down the centre of the road and covered with cloths. Chairs were brought out of the houses and arranged down each side. Use was now made of the precious items of food hoarded for just this purpose. Vases were filled with flowers picked from our gardens and set at intervals down the tables, which were soon laden with plates of food. This was a day that would never been seen again, although VJ Day ran it pretty close three months later.

Below: D-Day was 6 June, 1944, when Allied forces landed in Normandy to begin the liberation of Western Europe. Everyone hoped the war would soon be over. However, there were many fierce battles in Europe and in the Pacific war with Japan before the fighting stopped in 1945. The surrender of Japan on 15 August, 1945, finally ending the conflict that had torn families apart for six years and that would ultimately lead to these celebrations. Street parties were taking place the length and bredth of the country and Sheffield was no exception. This picture shows one such party taking place in Carlton Road in the Hillsborough area, near to the football ground. The joy was mirrored across the city as Sheffielders let their hair down. Amidst the celebrations there were also services of thanksgiving in churches, as people for the first time began to reflect on what had happened to loved ones and friends lost in the conflict. The picture is almost entirely women and children as many Sheffield wives and mothers had not heard from their menfolk for several years.

EVENTS & OCCASIONS

The carriage of Queen Victoria comes to rest in front of Sheffield Town Hall, on the occasion of the official opening. On either side of the entrance were two shaded platforms occupied by privileged spectators, while opposite were the guard of honour of the Hallamshire Volunteers. This visit on 21 May, 1897, was the first visit of a reigning Sovereign to the city. The ceremony at the Town Hall was said to have

The route taken by the Queen's carriages from the Midland station to the Town Hall, was Shea Street, Commercial Street, High Street, Fargate, and then around the building to Pinstone Street. In the Queen's carriage, Princess Christian sat by her side, and the Duke of Connaught sat opposite. The Queen seemed to be in excellent health and spirits and Her Majesty repeatedly acknowledged the acclamations of the people with evident pleasure.

Below: What better place to celebrate than at the Ladys Bridge Hotel in Bridge Street, next door to the Tennant Brothers Ltd Exchange Brewery. Also known as the Brewer On The Bridge, the Ladys Bridge Hotel was situated at 3, Bridge Street. The pub had been built in 1867 as the brewery tap for the Exchange Brewery, which had been established in 1852 by the Tennant brothers. The buildings had been lavishly decorated in honour of the visit of King Edward VII and Queen Alexandra to Sheffield in 1905. Large crowds had started to gather at the end of Bridge Street and into Waingate.

lasted ten minutes. A gold casket and key were presented to her Majesty, designed and manufactured by Messrs. Mappin and Webb, Royal Works in Sheffield. On a sunny day eager spectators lined the streets in their thousands to catch a glimpse of the Queen. As the afternoon wore on the excitement grew with the sound of bells clashing, bands playing, and flags waving,

'Long Live Our King and Queen' says the slogan on the side of this illuminated Sheffield tram, which had been decorated with lights for the visit of King Edward VII and Queen Alexandra to Sheffield in 1905. The car had previously been the popular highlight of a visit to Sheffield by General Kitchener, the victor of the Battle of Omdurman. According to contemporary accounts: "It is indeed a miracle of light, and a great credit to the officials who have prepared its fairy wonders for the delectation of the public... It would be difficult to estimate the number of juveniles it has kept out of bed after orthodox hours. In this respect there has been a pretty generous license all the week. If the King and Queen had no time to spare for the decorations - many of which by the way they must have seen before - the young people and our country visitors have feasted on them."

At the Coronation Pageant in Sheffield 1,500 children from local schools danced a programme of Morris, maypole and country dances in Bramall Lane football ground - the home of Sheffield United FC. The Coronation of King George VI took place at Westminster Abbey on 18 May, 1911. There was, of course, far more to the pageant than just Morris dancing: vast numbers of local folk participated in the vent with bands and displays from all sectors of Sheffield society attending the celebrations. Bramhall Lane was a regular venue for such displays, not least the Empire Day Pageant held in 1906. It was not until after the death of Queen Victoria, who died on 22 January, 1901, that Empire Day was first celebrated. The first 'Empire Day' took place on 24 May, 1902, the late Queen's birthday. Although not officially recognised as an annual event until 1916, many schools across the British Empire were celebrating it before then. Empire Day remained an essential part of the calendar for more than 50 years, celebrated by countless millions of children and adults alike, an opportunity to demonstrate pride in being part of the British Empire Political correctness, however, won the day when in 1958 Empire Day was re-badged as British Commonwealth Day. Still later in 1966 it became known as Commonwealth Day. The date of Commonwealth Day was also changed to 10 June, the official birthday of Queen Elizabeth II. The date was again changed in 1977 to the second Monday in March. Today, like Oak Apple Day and Waterloo Day, Empire Day seems all but forgotten.

Did you know?

In 1857 a collective of cricketers formed the world's first-ever official association football club, Sheffield F.C.

Below: A happy and smiling David Lloyd George, is seen here being carried in a chair by students at Sheffield University in October 1919. The then Prime Minister had just been made a Freeman of Sheffield. He was very vocal in his praise for the city's war effort. Between 1914 and 1919 it is estimated that Sheffield, produced 11 million shells, 7 million steel helmets, 3 million rifle barrels, 514,000 gun barrels, tubes and jackets, 212,000 tons of aeroplane steel and 16,650 guns. During the visit he was also given an honourary degree at Sheffield University. Lloyd George was a devout evangeliist and an icon of 20th century liberalism as the founder of the welfare state. He is regarded as having made a greater impact on British public life than any other 20th century leader, thanks to his leadership of the war effort, his post war role in reshaping Europe, and his introduction of Britain's social welfare system before the war. A substantive programme of social reform was introduced under Lloyd George's post war government. The Education Act 1918 raised the school leaving age to 14, increased the powers and duties of the Board of Education and introduced a system of day-continuation schools, which youths between the ages of 14 and 16 "could be compelled to attend for at least one day a week."

Right: Posing outside the Manor Baptist Church, in Prince of Wales Road, in May 1959, is that year's May Queen and her entourage. A May Queen is selected from a group of girls aged 13 and over by the young dancers. She returns the next year to crown the new May Queen and stays in the procession. Appointing a May Queen is an ancient British folk custom, one certainly pre-dating Christianity. Whether the ancient British pagans really sacrificed the May Queen to encourage a good harvest is, however, a matter of conjecture – perhaps no more than ancient Christian propaganda. We can be certain however that the May Queen of 1959 need have had no worries on that score. Today, these eleven youngsters must be all approaching, or well into, their sixties. Do they still remember that day we wonder?

Right: On 5 July, 1934, the Duchess of York visited Sheffield. Here she is pictured at the opening of the new records and treatment departments at the Royal Infirmary. Later that same day the Duchess also opened the Library and the Graves Art Gallery, as well as visiting the firms of Thos. Firth and John Brown. The 34-year-old Duchess was rather a minor royal in 1934. Two years later all that would change when her husband Prince George, the Duke of York, would unexpectedly ascend to the throne. The former Elizabeth Bowes-Lyon suddenly found herself not the Duchess of York but Queen Elizabeth, Empress of India, and mother of the heir to the throne, the Princess Elizabeth. But in 1934 that future was still undreamed of, not least that as the 'Queen Mum' the Duchess would live to see beyond the millennium.

Above: A charming picture of the King and Queen arriving in Sheffield, where they were received by the Mayor and Mayoress. After driving through the city, the King inaugurated the Ladybower Reservoir, in the Derwent Valley. The reservoir, which has a capacity of 6310 million gallons, is claimed to be the largest artificial reservoir within an earthwork embankment in the British Isles. It supplied the water needs of Derby, Leicester, Nottingham, Sheffield, and many centres in Derbyshire. King George VI and Queen Elizabeth can be seen walking up to the viaduct to perform the opening ceremony on 25 September, 1945.

Right and facing page: A series of pictures from the visit of Queen Elizabeth II and the Duke of Edinburgh on their two-day visit to Sheffield in October, 1954. They were greeted at the Town Hall by the Lord Mayor, Ald J H Bingham. Thousands lined the streets to gain the best vantage point to see the Royal visitors.

During the visit the Queen and Duke visited the English Steel Corporation where they saw first hand the city's

patients from Middlewood Hospital an uninterrupted view. Lunch was taken at the Town Hall and then the Royal party moved on to Hillsborough football ground, where 3,000 children impressed them by lining up on the pitch forming the words "Welcome to Sheffield".

The Queen and the Duke of Edinburgh also visited the University of Sheffield in order to inaugurate its Jubilee Session. No other reigning sovereign had visited the principal university buildings since King Edward VII opened them in 1905.

The visit ended on a high note at a reception given at Cutlers Hall, infront of the largest crowd High Street has ever seen. The Queen and the Duke of Edinburgh each received an appropriate gift as a memento of their visit to Sheffield. The tour was seen as a triumph and the Queen and Duke endeared themselves to the people of the city.

traditional industry, and in the Siemens melting shop they watched with interest as perspiring workers tapped 90 tons of molten steel.

In addition, they visited the City General Hospital in Herries Road, where they were greeted by young patients covered in blankets, and their devoted nurses.

Did you know?

Stainless steel or "rustless steel" was invented in 1912 by Harry Brearley who was born in Ramsden's Yard near the Wicker on 18 February, 1871.

Dr W H Hatfield of Sheffield is credited with the invention, in 1924, of 18/8 stainless steel and is thought to be the first person to use it on a motor car, applying the metal as a radiator and trim on his bullnose Morris Cowley.

The excited children were treated to more than a passing glimpse of the royal couple – their gleaming Rolls Royce slowed down to a crawl as it passed the flag waving supporters. It proved to be a special day for many more sick and disabled Sheffielders who were desperate to see the royal dignitaries. To facilitate this, panes of glass from the front windows were removed to give

GETTING AROUND

Below: The photograph shows the maiden trip of Sheffield's first electric tram car (No. 1), on South Street, Moor, on 5 September, 1899. On the driving platform are the Lord Mayor and members of the Tramway's Committee. Crowds are gathering to witness this special occasion at the bottom of The Moor, opposite the old Brunswick Wesleyan Chapel. These buildings eventually disappeared to make way for the new St. Mary's Gate Road. No. 1 tram was opening the Nether Edge route, formerly served for many years by the old horse-drawn trams that were introduced by the Sheffield Tramways Company in 1873, and taken over by the Corporation in 1896. A small tram shed was built at the Nether Edge terminus that opened in 1899.

Right: Obviously Sheffield Corporation staff get a free ride on the trams, as we can see at least six employees, not including the driver, on this 113 Tinsley tramcar. Sheffield Corporation (Sheffield City Council) took over the tramway system in July 1896. The Corporation's goal was to expand and mechanise the system. In 1899, the first electric tram ran between Nether Edge and Tinsley. By 1902 all the routes were electrified. By 1910 the network covered 39 miles. Happily for enthusiasts, as the last English city to give up its streetcars preservation beckoned for a number of Sheffield's finest trams at the newly established national tramway museum, including its last tramcar - number 510. Meanwhile 'The Last Time' inspired more than mere nostalgia. The late Rolling Stones guitarist, Brian Jones, was among those who made the pilgrimage to Sheffield to witness the end of an era on 8 October, 1960.

Bottom right: Looking towards Spital Hill, the Handsworth tram and tram shelter at the Wicker Arches was snapped by the cameraman, in 1909. Railway bridge number 134 crosses Wicker Road at the western end of Sheffield Victoria station. Selling advertising

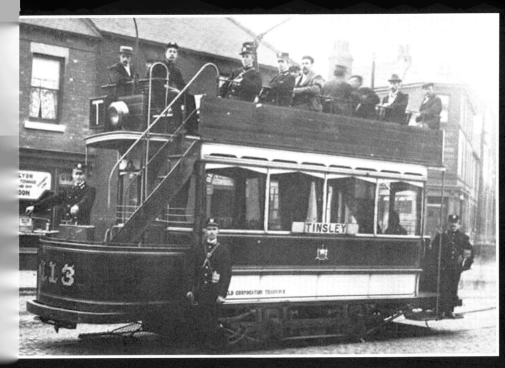

space on bridges was a nice little earner for railway companies; here the adverts on the bridge promote the Empire theatre, and more prominently 'Berrys Lion Ales'. Founded in 1829 by Thomas Berry, by 1884 the Sheffield brewery owned a tied estate of upwards of 100 public houses It employed 100 workers, and the annual output was in the region of 50,000 barrels of beer. Sixty years later Berry's was taken over by Tennant's Brewery, which continued the famous line of 'Lion Ales' for many years.

Right: On Monday, 26 August, 1907, the Sheffield Daily Independent headline read: 'APPALLING SMASH NEAR MOSCAR, MOTOR CHAR-A-BANC DASHED INTO WALL. THREE KILLED, MANY OTHERS INJURED. SICKENING SCENES'. Under the headlines the paper revealed that a char-a-banc had been proceeding past a carriage and a pair of horses when it hit a telegraph pole, causing it to skid and then crash into a stone wall. A man with a little boy, aged seven on his knees was killed instantly; another man was killed by being thrown from the vehicle. A person who was passing by on the road tried to run away but was caught by the crashing vehicle and pushed through a stone wall. He suffered a broken right leg and severe head injuries. With no such thing as driving tests, MOTs or power-assisted brakes the roads were far more dangerous then than they are today.

Below: Some folk get quite obsessed with the minutiae of passenger transport, whether it is train spotting or buses. The aficionado will want to know that these buses are numbers 180, 14F and 28, though in fact the real enthusiast will probably already know that – and know the livery colour, date of delivery and the name of the both drivers and conductors! A cameraman captured this trio of Leyland buses for posterity in 1929; they have been taken into the paintshop at the Queen's Road Work to have their exteriors buffed up before they take to the road for the first time. These buses were in service from 1929 to 1935, though the real expert will no doubt say 'ah well, yes, but...' and provide more details that we could ever have dreamed of. Worthy of note are the tram tracks on the floor, which the motorbuses can happily ignore.

Facing page: Two differing images showing a view of Firth Park roundabout in the late 1940s. The main picture from August 1947 shows all kind of vehicles trying to thread their way through the line of trams, passing through the centre of the roundabout on Firth Park Road. The single-decker bus is picking up from the bottom of Bellhouse Road. The photograph looks to have been taken from on of the dormer windows above the shops in Stubbin Lane. The second image is from approximately two years later, in 1949, and shows a lorry in the foreground on Firth Park roundabout, with Sicey Avenue behind. On the left is The United Methodist Church, built in 1911, and further up Sicey Avenue is the Paragon Cinema.

Local readers, may remember it was the first Sheffield cinema to be built in the sound era, in October 1934. The cinema, designed by Robert Cawkwell, was open for less than 30 years, closing in February 1962. The building was later demolished and became the site of a bowling alley and supermarket.

The roundabout itself is unique, in as much as it has continued to have the preserved tram track running through the centre, in the theme of the old tram turnaround point from the 1950s. In addition, when the entrance to Firth Park was refurbished, decorative gates were added.

This is a view along Blonk Street looking towards Victoria Station. Access to the station was via Victoria Station Road, which paralleled Furnival Road before the latter plunged beneath the station to emerge on the other side. Adjoining the station at the end of Victoria Station Road was the Royal Victoria Hotel. Engineered by Joseph Locke, the Sheffield, Ashton-under-Lyne and Manchester Railway linking Manchester and Sheffield opened in 1845. Originally, this line terminated at the Bridgehouses station about 0.7 miles (1 km) to the west of the future Victoria station. In 1847, the Sheffield, Ashton-

under-Lyne and Manchester Railway merged with two other railway companies to form the Manchester, Sheffield and Lincolnshire Railway. The station received a new frontage in 1908 and took on great importance when the line through the Pennines—known as the Woodhead Route after the long Woodhead Tunnel on it which was electrified for freight purposes after World War II. The electrification of the line reached Sheffield Victoria by 1954, reducing the journey time to Manchester to 56 minutes. This was the first main line in the UK to be electrified. Although the 1950s saw services at the station reach their peak, this period also

marked the beginning of its decline as road traffic grew and the mills closed. In 1965 the second Beeching Report recommended that the Sheffield to Manchester service be consolidated; after much local wrangling British Railways favoured the Hope Valley Line which was slower and not electrified but served more local communities. In 1967, plans were announced to withdraw passenger services along the Woodhead route. Following public outcry, an enquiry was launched that took two years to be completed. Eventually the enquiry backed British Rail's plans and passenger services were withdrawn from the line on 5 January, 1970. The last train to Victoria station, an enthusiasts' special, arrived at 00:44 on 5 January and from that point the station was closed. The station re-opened very briefly in 1972 for diverted trains while Sheffield (Midland) station was closed for re-signalling.

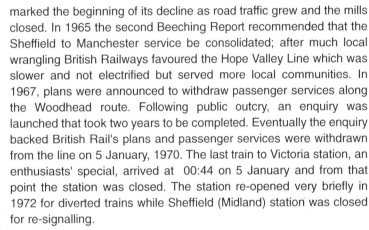

WORKING LIFE

Below: Ah those were the days! Or were they? Smoke and steam billow dramatically over the Sheffield skyline. Who could count the number of chimneys in Sheffield in 1947 when this scene was captured by the camera? Who could count the number of steam locomotives pulling the coal trains in and out of Sheffield each day? It's hard not to feel nostalgia for the days when even if blindfolded you could taste the very air of Sheffield and know you were at the beating heart of a giant industrial centre. The downside of course was smog – that awful combination of smoke and fog that brought in its wake chronic respiratory diseases. Asthma and bronchitis were the everyday lot of Sheffield folk, diseases that each winter took their dreadful harvest of lives. The Clean Air Acts of the 1950s, the switch from domestic coal fires to gas and electricity in the 1960s and an increased awareness of industrial pollution has transformed the environment.

Did you know?

Over half of the world's surgical blades are made in Sheffield.

Right, facing page: The steel industry in Sheffield dates to at least the 14th century and was even noted for the production of

knives by Geoffrey Chaucer in his book The Canterbury Tales. Before 1500 watermills were adapted to grinding tools and the cutlery trade boomed. In 1624 The Company of Cutlers in Hallamshire was formed to oversee the trade. In 1740 Benjamin Huntsman discovered the crucible technique for steel manufacture, at his workshop in the district of Handsworth. This process had an enormous impact on the quantity and quality of steel production and was only made obsolete, a century later. Sheffield continued to gain an international reputation for metallurgy and steel-making. It was this industry that established it as one of England's main industrial cities during the 18th, 19th and 20th centuries. This industry used Sheffield's unique combination of local Iron, Coal and water power supplied by the local rivers. This fuelled a massive growth in the city's population that expanded from just over 60,000 in 1801 to a peak of 577,050 in 1951.

Did you know?

As early as the fourteenth century, Sheffield was known as a place for the production of knives. It was even mentioned in Chaucer's Canterbury Tales.

Above and below: In this view we can see the shopfront of J Preston, chemist, located at 105 Barker's Pool. Older readers in particular will be able to recall the name of Prestons, as their origins can be traced back to the early 1830s. Aside of the traditional chemist shop, the company supplied products to laboratories in many fields including the city's vibrant steel industry. J Preston Limited also had its own glass shop with a team of glassblowers which produced specialist laboratory glassware to order. In the second photograph, below, is an example of one of the glassblowing team, Vera Mary Stone, who is seen here as a 16-year-old blowing glass at Prestons during World War Two in June

1942. It is still possible to see how this chemists shop may have looked inside, as the fittings were given to Weston Park Museum after the company ended a long history as a local retailer and moved to Netherthorpe Road, in 1987.

Top, facing page: In the 1920s the Sheffield Gas Company was delivering sacks of coke to customers all across Sheffield, and even further afield. Though today household gas comes from under the North Sea and other natural gas fields, it was not always thus. 'Town gas' was manufactured from coal. When heated in large ovens, coal gave off gas which could thenbe piped into huge, round

smokeless fuel and an essential ingredient for smelting steel. Natural gas is odourless and the distinctive smell is added artificially. There was no such problem with town gas! Though originally private businesses, all gas and electric companies would eventually be nationalised.

Below: Looking very proud and posing for the camera are policewomen Hazel Layne and Dorothy Elliott, prior to climbing into their brand new 100mph police car, which gave them the distinction of becoming

gasometers before distribution to customers. The heated coal also gave out 'coal tar' which could be collected and used in the chemical industry. What is left of coal after this process is grey brittle coke, almost pure carbon, an ideal

Sheffield's first all-girls squad car team. The Sheffield force had equipped the ton-up girls with a new £1,800 squad car specially designed for high-speed chases in October 1969.

The Wolf Safety Lamp Company (Wm. Maurice) Ltd
An Illuminating Story

It was a rare privilege to be visited by His Royal Highness Prince Edward, the Earl of Wessex, as part of the Wolf Safety Lamp Company centenary celebrations on Wednesday, 25 January, 2012. A privilege perhaps; but an accolade well deserved. For over a century, led by some remarkable individuals, the Wolf Safety Lamp Company founded by William Maurice has more than earned its place amongst the pantheon of local, national and international businesses as a major miners and safety lamp manufacturer.

The founder's daughter, Monica Maurice, was a member of the company for over sixty years, and a director for fifty. She became one of the most respected engineers in her field. When she was asked how she so skillfully competed in what was traditionally a man's world, her response was simple, 'by being better'.

Monica's son, John Jackson, now Chairman, successfully diversified its product range for applications in the petrochemicals, explosive atmospheres and fire-fighting safety markets. The founder's great grandsons, Alex and Miles, continue the family tradition.

The family owned business was acquired under licence by William Maurice in 1912 from Friemann & Wolf GmbH, of Zwickau, in Germany.

Had it not been for Carl Wolf and his patented invention of 'the benzene' fuelled re-lightable flame safety lamp, in 1882, Wolf Safety of Sheffield would not exist. Equally, had Wolf, himself the son of a miner, not met Heinrich Friemann who assisted him with his patent application, and then financed the formation of the manufacturing company, Friemann & Wolf would not have become giants of lamp production, dominating the world of mine lighting across the globe for decades.

Top left: *William Maurice at a conference at the Royal Agricultural Hall, London, in the late 1930s.* **Above:** *Wolf Safety Lamps on display in November 1937.* **Below:** *The Saxon Road works in 1933.*

Back Row L-R: George Fazackerley, Frank Hobson, Ron Lamb, Un-Known, Malcome Street, H. Klauze, Herbert Fischer, Rowland Nelson, Rueben ("Pop") Bower, Jack Haslam, Eric Neil
Middle Row: L-R: Irene, Evelyn Howlett, Mrs Bower, Esme Downes, Alfred Hall, Evelyn Street, Harry Farnsworth, Un-Known, Doris Stoneham, Sylvia Price, Joan Eastwood, Margaret Clarke
Front Row L-R: Ray Forster, Madge, George Laidler, Paul Roedel, Monica Maurice, William Maurice, Robert Cumming, Fred Walker, Ivy Tear, Cecil Whiting

By 1907, Friemann & Wolf were producing numerous models of spirit, oil and acetylene miners' lamps, and some of the very first electric mine lamps. The year 1915 marked the production of the one millionth Wolf Miners' Lamp.

With the imposition of the 'Trading with the Enemy Amendment Act' in 1916, William Maurice was able to acquire the entire British business of The Wolf Safety Lamp Company. A working relationship was reformed in the 1920s and continued until the outbreak of the Second World War.

By the late 1920s, Wolf in Germany had developed a refined version of the nickel cadmium accumulator safety lamp, together with a powerful compressed air driven turbine lamp designed for coal face lighting, a type of product which is still in production in Sheffield today.

The roles of 1912 were now reversed. The original rigid agreement was long

in the past and the titans of world lamp making were happy to be producing prototype and pre-production Wolf lamps, modified to William Maurice's own patented designs.

In 1905, when William was General Mine Manager at Hucknall Collieries, he installed the first exhaust steam turbo-alternator generator to be used in a British mine, and in 1908, added a booster motor generator and equalising battery charging system, a combination unique in the history of engineering development. At the time it was the only example of its kind in the world. He was also the first to develop the thin coal seams of the Leen Valley Colliery, and the first to make use of electric coal-cutters in the area.

*Top: Outside the Saxon Road works, Spring 1938. **Left:** Monica Maurice and Paul Roedel, who was the works manager, pictured in March 1939.*

papers were published in the Institute of Mining Engineers Journal. He also built an impressive library of first editions by contemporary authors. Over the years he collected and commissioned paintings, prints and drawings on mining subjects. He was fascinated by the culture and traditions of miners, as referred to and recorded in prose, poetry and song. From the years 1924 to 1942, he collected together a significant amount of material from which he compiled a 'Pitman's Anthology', but due to lack of contemporary appeal it was never published. William Maurice also recognised the value of catalogues, promotions and trade marks.

He passionately believed that electricity, both for lighting and machinery, was the only way forward and co-founded the Association of Mining Electrical Engineers, and was elected first president.

William Maurice was born in Macclesfield in 1872, and originally embarked upon a career in chemistry and metallurgy, but in 1890 he joined John Davis & Son, of Derby, as an articled electrical engineering student. In 1892-1893, he installed electrical equipment in the mines at Kimberley, in South Africa, on behalf of Davis of Derby. In 1894, he was appointed electrical engineer at Swanwick Collieries, Alfreton, and subsequently became assistant to the manager, under whom he qualified as a colliery manager. By 1899, he was appointed manager of the Babbington Coal Company's Tibshelf New Colliery, where he remained until 1903 before moving to Hucknall.

The wolf's head emblem, facing ahead, first registered as a trade mark by the Leeds Company, was redesigned for the catalogue of 1914, but in the 1920s and up to 1936, the design reverted back to the Friemann & Wolf emblem of the wolf's head in a circle, lamp in mouth, facing to the left. With the new era of the Model Factory on line in 1935, the wolf's head was redesigned, this time facing to the right, used up to 1959. From 1960 to the early 1980s, the Company logo was taken from a brass casting of a wolf's head, face on, but without a lamp in its mouth. From then, until the current logo, a modernised version of the pre-war wolf was used. The new logo echoed something of the tradition of all these emblems, but with the

*Top left: The new, clean, open and well-lit spaces of the Saxon Road works in 1934. **Centre:** Three examples of the wolf's head logos used by the company. **Below:** A demonstration of the Wolf Safety Lamp range to lamp room managers.*

At Hucknall that year, William married Helen Laura Wheeler. Monica, the first of three daughters was born there in 1908, followed by Cynthia a year later and Pauline in 1914, by which time the family was established in Sheffield. In 1920, William Maurice purchased a 20 year lease on Park Grange, part of the Norfolk estates on the hillside above Farm Lane and Granville Road, long since demolished for replacement with high-rise flats. The large Victorian mansion house was set in acres of farmland with panoramic views of the city.

This era was the heyday for William Maurice and the Company. Many of his

head tilted upwards, as though scenting the air for new opportunities.

The business, which also included William Maurice's Federation Lamp Co. Ltd., relocated to South Street, Park, behind the Sheffield Midland Railway Station in 1923. During those early days William Maurice registered 10 patented improvements to acetylene, flame and air turbo safety mining lamps.

Meanwhile, an indicator of William Maurice's liberal attitude, rare in the realms of engineering at that time, was that his three daughters were educated at Bedales, a progressive co-educational boarding school in Hampshire. Monica became head girl in 1926. After school she studied languages at the Sorbonne in Paris, and then Engineering at Hamburg University. Her original intention was to become a dress designer and her passion for clothes remained with her throughout her life. Many of her dresses and hats from the period are now in the Victoria & Albert Museum.

However, with the realisation that no-one else in the family would succeed her father, Monica switched her attentions to engineering. In 1930, Monica joined the company, becoming a director in 1934. Her career lasted more than sixty years.

The year 1933 was a momentous one for the company, with the purchase of the industrial site still occupied today, known as Saxon Road Works, in Heeley. The buildings were completely reconstructed and installed with new electrically operated machinery, the first in Sheffield, creating a Model Factory. The first floor offices were supplied with Pilkington tiled fireplaces, modern office furniture and filing systems commissioned in oak and ebony, with steel frame and leather upholstered chairs, all to Monica Maurice's own designs. The entire building was equipped with an internal telephone system and maximised the use of daylight in the offices and on the factory floor. On each first floor windowsill was a carefully tended window box of flowers.

By 1934, with an increased workforce, the new factory was in full production. Two years later, Monica Maurice organised a conference for the Women's Engineering Society at Sheffield University, which included a tour of the company's 'Model Factory of the New Electric Age'. That year, Amy Johnson, the world famous aviatrix, was President of the Society.

Monica was fluent in French and German. On a number of occasions she presented papers on her father's behalf to the Congres International des Mines in Liege, and at similar conferences held in Berlin and Karlsruhe.

Top The Women's Engineering Society at Wolf's premises in 1936. Monica Maurice is right of centre and Amy Johnson is on her left. **Left:** *Monica in her chain-gang Fraser Nash in 1935.* **Below:** *Wolf's stand at the National Coalboard Exhibition in Wrexham between February and March 1951.*

In 1938 Monica had met Canadian doctor, Arthur Jackson, and after a whirlwind romance they were married in the Chapel on the Bridge, in Rotherham. They settled down to domestic life at Ash Croft in Wentworth village. Arthur Jackson purchased a General Medical Practice in Woodhouse, on the east side of Sheffield, and the family moved into Newton Croft, a Georgian House in the centre of the village. Both were active in local events. Not surprisingly, some of the company's newly recruited workforce lived in Woodhouse and Bob Graves, a much respected local Scout Master, ran a 'taxi' service to and from Saxon Road in his converted army ambulance for many years.

Like her father, she was also an active member of the Institute of Mining Engineers and AMEME, (later to incorporate Mining Mechanical Engineers), and in due course was elected a member of the Institute of Electrical Engineers (IEE), and a fellow of the Institute of Quality Assurance. In her spare time she learned to fly, often with Joy Davison, another well known aviatrix against whom she also raced cars - Monica driving her Fraser Nash and Joy in her faster but less nimble Isotta Fraschini.

George Brough, of motorcycle fame, gave Monica the occasional drive in his works supercharged Brough Superior hill climbing car. Post-war, she ran a Brough Superior, as did her husband, followed by a Mark VI Bentley in which she drove her three children to and from boarding school in Hampshire. Latterly Monica ran a yellow Aston Martin, whose open exhausts could be heard long before it was seen!

During the war years, the company continued making miners lamps, but as a further part of the war effort they produced aircraft fuel pumps. During this period, Monica served on a number of International Standards Committees, including one for standardising screw threads and recounting the trials and tribulations during the latter part of the war, in dealing with the Russians. A daughter was born in 1941 and twin sons in 1943. In pre-war visits to Germany she had developed a special friendship with the Wolf family, and in particular Carl Wolf's daughter Erika. When she was invited in 1947 to participate in a British Intelligence Objectives survey team to assess the war damage and reclamation of the German battery industry, she leaped at the opportunity. With the rank of full colonel heading a team of six engineers, she covered dozens of sites in all four occupied zones. During this visit she re-met her close friend Erika, but in much changed circumstances.

*Top left: Celebrations with the staff of the Company on Monica's 50 years with Wolf Safety in 1980. **Above:** Monica Maurice with her OBE, with her husband, Arthur Jackson, and their daughter, Willa and son, John, in 1975. **Left:** A wolf Rechargeable Torch in use by Grampian Fire & Rescue Service.*

The 1950s was about rebuilding lost markets, and the company's survival entailed a combination of orders from the National Coal Board and the export of safety lamps, in particular to South Africa and South America. With the death of William Maurice, in 1951, and the rapid decline of the coal industry, key sales in the next two decades lay in contracts with emerging oil and gas industries.

The pattern of trading and commerce was also changing, with specialist distributors and agents being appointed worldwide. In 1970, Tom Fallon, an avid American collector of mining lamps, called on Monica Maurice for advice about a book he was planning to write on the history of mining

lamps. Two years later a telegram was received from Tom which read; 'I have just today registered Safety Lamp of Houston and hopefully I am now your first main agent in North America'. That was the start of a long and fruitful relationship.

Arthur Jackson retired in 1972 and he and Monica moved to the Derbyshire village of Ashford in the Water.

Without doubt one of the company's brightest moments was when Monica Maurice, known throughout Sheffield, the coal fields and the world of safety engineering as 'The Lady of the Lamp', was presented with the OBE by HM The Queen in 1975. Monica passed away in 1995.

The future of The Wolf Safety Lamp Co. of Sheffield looks bright. Today, John Jackson is Chairman, Alex Jackson is Managing Director and Miles Jackson Director of sales and marketing. William Maurice would have been very proud to know that his great grandsons are taking his company forward into its second hundred years stronger and brighter than ever.

*Top left and left: Wolf Tank Lighting Kit. **Above:** A Wolf Portable Searchlight. **Below:** A 2012 Wolf company photograph.*

Back Row L-R: John Barraclough, Neal Jepson, Phillip Smith, Graham Roberts, Norman Cox, Ewelina Rozek, Mark Cocking, Christine Lindley, Mark Gurnhill, Andrew Kempton
Middle Row L-R: Lindsey Copley-Dunn, Kirsty Carr, Helen Reaney, Maria Dyson, Louise Marsden, Maria Doyle, Karen Moore, Valerie Bell, Anthony Ramsden, Gina France, Cheryl McCormick, Peter Stanley, Anne Harrison, Kelly Clarkson, Lisa Turner
Front Row L-R: Michael Morley, Alison Lawton, Audrey Giles, Miles Jackson, Ian Tinker, John Jackson, Alex Jackson, Jeff Kershaw, Pascale Coates, Jeff Crossland

Sheffield Assay Office
The Mark of Quality

There has been an Assay Office in Sheffield since 1773 when local silversmiths joined forces with Birmingham petitioners to ask Parliament for their own Assay Office. Despite fierce opposition from the London Goldsmiths' Company, an Act was passed granting Sheffield the right to assay silver.

The earliest known piece of Sheffield silver is a pocket watch from about 1720. What had put Sheffield on the world map, however, had been Thomas Boulsover's invention of Sheffield Plate. This was the fusing of silver onto copper and was first used to make silver buttons. By the mid-1760s a number of Old Sheffield Plate manufacturers were also making silver tableware, but products had to be sent to London for hallmarking.

By 1773, there were some 468 persons working in the plated and sterling silver trades in Sheffield and a local Assay Office was urgently needed.

An Act of Parliament appointed 30 local men as 'Guardians of the Standard Wrought Plate within the Town of Sheffield' to supervise the work of the Office. By restricting the number of Guardians who were silversmiths to fewer than 10, Parliament made sure that the Office was run for the benefit of the consumer rather than the manufacturer. The day to day running of the Office was entrusted to an Assay Master who had to take an oath before the Master of the Royal Mint and enter into a bond for £500. The Office was to be non-profit making and its running costs were to be met by the hallmarking charges paid by the manufacturers.

The 1773 Act empowered Sheffield to use a crown as its Town mark. The story goes that this was because Birmingham and Sheffield petitioners for the Act met at the Crown and Anchor, an inn situated off The Strand in London, and that each town adopted one of these signs as its mark.

Top left: A coffee pot made by silversmiths Matthew Fenton, Richard Creswick and William Watson sent to the Sheffield Assay Office for marking in 1773. **Above:** The four markings which make up this hallmark read from left to right, Tudor & Leader (Sponsor's Mark), Sterling Silver (Standard Mark), Sheffield (Town Mark), and 1773 (Date Letter). **Below left:** Candlesticks made by Samuel Roberts, 1773. **Below:** The Assay Office, Fargate, 1795-1881.

In addition to the crown, a date mark too would be used: in Sheffield an old English letter E was chosen as the first date-letter for hallmarking. After 1903, when Sheffield was finally allowed to assay and mark gold as well as silver, Sheffield had two town marks - the crown for silver and a rose for gold.

Originally Sheffield had been given the exclusive right to mark all silver goods produced within a 20 mile radius of Sheffield. After a second Sheffield Act of 1784 the Office also had the right to keep a Register of all makers' marks on plated silverwares made within a 100 mile radius.

For the first 11 years the Office struggled to survive. By using mass-production methods for stamping out thin silver Sheffield made very light wares. Assaying, however, was charged for by weight. Over 100 knife handles could be marked for only a shilling (5p) - a price which did not reflect the time and effort involved. An Act of 1784 allowed for small articles to be charged for per item rather than by weight.

The first Assay Office was located in Norfolk Street and its first Assay Master was a Londoner, Daniel Bradbury. The office only opened on Mondays and Thursdays, although Bradbury was permitted to open on a third day for private assays. In 1774 the Office moved to a court off Norfolk Street 'lately occupied by Thomas Boulsover' the inventor of Sheffield Plate.

By 1795 the Office had moved again, this time to a brand new building on Fargate.

When in 1880 the Fargate premises were needed for road widening, the Guardians acquired a new site in Leopold Street, where the Offices would remain until 1958.

Leopold Street would witness some remarkable events. When the Indian Maharaja Raj Rama Bhawaur Singh wanted a new bedroom suite he wanted it made in silver. Sheffield silversmiths Mappin and Webb were commissioned to make the furniture. This turned out to be quite a problem for the Assay Office. The Maharaja's silver four-poster bed, weighing more than a ton, was manhandled through one of the Assay Office's windows whose frame had to be removed before the bed could be taken into the marking hall.

Above: A 9ct gold and steel folding penknife made by Needham Brothers, Sheffield, hallmarked Sheffield 1915.
Left: Arnold Foster marking salvers. Below: Leopold Street Assay Office 1881 - 1958.

extra work was spent on alterations and to build the Goldsmiths' Wing creating more marking space - the foundation stone being laid in October 1978 by Ian Threfall, the Prime Warden of the Goldsmith's Company. Meanwhile, the Office bought the former Willow Tree pub next door and fitted it out for offices and marking. The Office also bought the Charleston Works, in Orange Street, adjacent to the Willow Tree. In 1983, Sir Frederick Dainton, later Prime Warden of the Goldsmiths' Company, laid the foundation stone of the Guardians' Hall. The new building was officially opened by Her Majesty Queen Elizabeth II in December 1986.

The bed, along with the rest of the silver bedroom suite, which included chamber pots, a sideboard, dressing table, four occasional tables, six easy chairs, half a dozen single chairs, two couches and ottomans, taken together formed the largest set of items ever handled by the Sheffield Assay Office. Before the Second World War some million and a quarter ounces of silver passed through the Office each year. By 1958, however, this had fallen to 300,000 ounces. Silver simply went out of fashion. In the old days when there was a new Cunard liner or the Canadian Pacific railways opened a new chain of hotels they all wanted their silver tea services and the like, but now demand began to fall as stainless steel and electroplate replaced silver in many applications. Several of the largest local firms closed and it seemed as though the only people still making silverware were skilled craft-workers. The Office moved once more, this time to a much smaller building in Portobello Street.

After the Hallmarking Act was passed in 1973 the nature of the work submitted to the Assay Office changed. Goods from all over the United Kingdom and abroad came to be assayed. The extra workload made redevelopment necessary - at first within the existing building to streamline the laboratories and provide more marking space. In 1973, Jack Cheetham made some cufflinks in which the hallmark was a necessary and important part of the decoration; Jack Spencer adapted that idea and used the largest size of hallmark as decoration on a range of gold and silver jewellery. 'Dogtag' pendants became phenomenally popular. The income from this

The Office has continued to adapt to its customers' needs and was soon creating even more laboratory space and streamlining the hallmarking process. In 1997 laser marking was introduced for hollow articles such as necklaces, watch cases and bangles which would have been damaged by traditional methods. Over a quarter of a million such items were marked in 1999.

Top left: The original building and Guardians' Hall on Portobello Street, home to Sheffield Assay Office from 1958-2008. *Above:* HRH The Duke of Edinburgh observes the marking of the Grand National Trophy by Arnold Foster and Martyn Brammer on his visit in 1973. *Left:* The Sheffield Assay Office's Bi-centenary Rose Bowl by Keith Tyssen.

Sheffield Analytical Services Laboratory not only tests precious metals, the team provide a variety of analytical services to medical, dentistry and environmental companies, from testing health care products to mineral analysis. The Assay Office also provide independent assays for bullions companies, this work complements the traditional assaying and hallmarking work.

January 1999 saw the introduction of new (and lower) standards for gold, silver and platinum to permit free competition within the European Community. For the first time the date-letter became voluntary rather than compulsory, and the sterling lion mark and crown gold mark also became optional. Today, all goods are marked with their standard of fineness in parts per thousand and it is no longer possible to distinguish between British and foreign made

Initially, any surpluses made by the Office had to be used solely for prosecuting those who broke the law on hallmarking. However, by the beginning of the 20th century, when the local silver industry was at its height, the Office was making a large profit. As a result, a new Act of 1906 granted the right for some of the surplus to be spent on providing a collection of books and objects relating to the gold and silver industry, to promoting technical education in Sheffield, especially for the gold and silver industry, and to provide support to charities.

articles. An additional special mark for the Millennium was also introduced to be used on any item made between January 1999 and December 2000 at the manufacturer's request. This captured the public imagination and increased the sale of precious metal wares significantly.

In the 21st century the workload has continued to grow. In 2001, 13 million articles were assayed and marked in Sheffield. More staff were taken on and the building extended yet again, this time to create a new top floor for Guardians' Hall providing comfortable staff accommodation, whilst the old staff room was converted to make more room for marking. An extension was opened on 11 April, 2002, by HRH the Duke of Kent, the third Royal visitor to the Office in 30 years. Another special mark to commemorate HM Queen Elizabeth II's Golden Jubilee was used for one year only in 2002.

Top: Her Majesty Queen Elizabeth II signs the visitors book in the boardroom onlooked by the Guardians and their partners, December 1986. Left: Rose Ganley. Laser marking is widely used for marking traditional, standard hallmarks onto precious metal but it is also an ideal process for clearly and accurately marking a range of logos, signatures and serial numbers for decorative, promotional or engineering and industrial purposes. Below: The Sheffield Assay Office Millennium Punchbowl.

Since then the Office has built up a large specialised library and a collection of silver, mainly made in Sheffield. The Office has also sponsored various competitions to encourage local crafts people and most recently financed a fully equipped workshop unit at Persistence Works for metalwork and jewellery graduates starting out in business. In addition the Office is a corporate member of the Millennium Galleries, where the splendid Millennium Punch Bowl is on display. The Office has also secured the future of Bradbury's Book of Hallmarks by taking over its publication on licence from the Bradbury family. This handy pocket reference book has been in print since 1927. Originally compiled by Frederick Bradbury, one of the descendants of the first Sheffield Assay Master Daniel Bradbury, with assistance from Bernard Watson, Assay Master 1898-1941, the book was in danger of going out of print but this new partnership ensures its survival into the 21st century.

The Assay Office is highly active in promoting local skills. The Starter Studio Programme is a two year rolling programme for early-career silversmiths and jewellers who have access to a fully equipped space, business support, mentoring and technical expertise as well as exhibition and commission opportunities. It has been in existence since 2002 and has supported over 20 young makers to date.

The Little Gems commissions is a project started in 2004 to develop new silversmithing talent in Sheffield and to continue the city's longstanding tradition of metalworking expertise and creativity. The project gives up-and-coming makers a unique opportunity to see their designs join the work made by some of the UK's leading silversmiths in the city's nationally significant metalwork collections. The Sheffield Assay Office has to date commissioned 18 of the new Little Gems pieces, created by talented early-career silversmiths.

In 2007, the introduction of the mixed-metal hallmark as a result of new Hallmarking legislation created new opportunities for the jewellery industry, and offered consumers a more accurate description of the items they purchased. That same year Assay Master Ashley Carson and members of his team gathered together to watch Colonel Roger Inman OBE, a former Chairman of the Assay Office, lay the foundation stone of a new building, Guardians' Hall, in Beulah Street, Hillsborough.

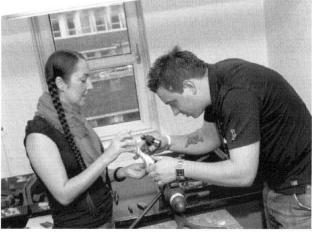

Top: In 2008 Sheffield Assay Office asked designer Katey Felton to design and make her own unique punch cup. Taking inspiration from the Sheffield hallmark she produced this piece entitled, 'Yorkshire Rose'. **Centre left:** Marking the last items at Portobello Road. **Left:** Assay Master Ashley Carson leads the way in transporting the old panels to the new Assay Office. **Above:** Christina Spencer has the first piece marked at Sheffield Assay's new Beulah Road, Hillsborough, premises.

The old building at Portobello Street in the centre of Sheffield had featured beautifully crafted oak panels, each bearing the date mark for every year of the Assay Office's history since 1773. The panels made the short journey across the city, where they were installed in 2008 when the Duke of Kent officially opened the new Sheffield Assay Office.

In 2010 palladium joined silver, gold and platinum as the fourth recognised precious metal to bear a Sheffield hallmark. Between July 2011 and October 2012 palladium, silver, gold, and platinum, upon request, would be applied with a special hallmark commemorating the Diamond Jubilee of Her Majesty Queen Elizabeth II. The chosen mark depicts a young Queen Elizabeth wearing an oversized crown in a diamond shaped surround

Today's Assay Master is Ashley Carson, who started work at the Office in 1977 as a teenage assistant in the marking hall. A local boy who attended Jordanthorpe School, Ashley's first job was

sweeping the floor and cleaning his boss's car. Continuing his education at Chesterfield College studying silversmithing, Ashley worked his way up the ranks to become, in 1993, Assay Master at the age of just 32, the youngest Master in the Assay Office's long history.

Some 240 years since it opened, Sheffield's Assay Office still protects customers and manufacturers alike, maintaining the City's reputation for integrity and efficiency. Although proud of its history its staff have always been keen to move with the times and to use the latest technology to satisfy its customers' needs - ensuring the very best of the past meets seamlessly with the best of the present.

Top left and top right: The Duke of Kent officially opens the new Sheffield Assay Office (above) in November 2008. **Above left:** *Two of Sheffield Assay's Little Gems commissions in 2011. An aperture bowl by Drew Sutherland and pepper grinder by Sally Cox.* **Left and right:** *A special Little Gems commission for the Queens Diamond Jubilee. Designed by Alexander Kerrison it carries the special commemorative hallmark pictured left. Entitled Carafe it is a combination of lead crystal glass wrapped in Britannia & Sterling silver.*

Edwin Jagger
The World's Finest Shave

which began life in a small workshop in the cellar of Neil's terrace house.

There he started to produce shaving razors manufactured from components shaped, honed and polished by a carefully selected group of Sheffield master craftsmen. The idea of producing razors, handmade in Sheffield came after Neil Jagger bought an Italian designed and built razor that looked good but didn't perform well and was badly constructed.

Using his extensive knowledge of hand-manufactured silver dinner services and cutlery, Jagger commissioned Sheffield craftsmen to manufacture components for a new range of handmade razors.

Neil Jagger was born in 1959 and brought up in the mining village of Old Ollerton, Nottinghamshire. Neil, the son of a headmaster, developed a keen eye for design, line and form and at the age of 14 had already filled his parents' garage with a woodworking bench and

*Left: Neil Jagger – Founder. **Above:** The Chatsworth Barley Chrome Razor, Elegant flawless handles are precision hand carved with decorative patterns, creating an impressive choice within the Edwin Jagger Collection. **Below:** The recently restored Shepherds wheel – A former water-powered grinding workshop. Situated on the Porter Brook in Sheffield, it is one of the earliest known wheels used to generate power for grinding blades in the city.*

Situated in the heart of Sheffield, Cavendish Works is the home of Edwin Jagger Ltd, an internationally renowned company with firm foundations in a city famous for its hand forged blades, specialist steels, sterling silverware and cutlery all hand crafted by some of the most skilled craftsmen in the world.

This family-owned and run business was set up 25 years ago specifically to design and manufacture high quality shaving accessories using the traditional skills of the city. Today, the business is a leader in its field with a name recognised around the world for excellence.

Edwin Jagger supplies more than 2,500 specialist retailers including gift shops, tobacconists, pharmacies and some of the world's finest flagship department stores including Harrods, Selfridges, Fortnum & Mason and Liberty with a selection of more than 700 exclusive Edwin Jagger products.

That's a huge leap forward for a company formed in 1988 by Neil Edwin Jagger who took his middle name from his grandfather and passed it to his business

tools and spent many hours building furniture and restoring the wooden hull of a yacht. School introduced Neil to the world of design, technical drawing, metalwork and engineering. In his spare time Neil could be found tinkering in the school's workshops developing his machining and engineering skills.

In 1976, at the age of 17, Neil moved to Sheffield, a city steeped in the traditions of cutlery, traditional metalwork and silversmithing. After completing his studies in silversmithing, metalwork, maths and physics, he took a summer job in one of Sheffield's finest silverware factories.

He was entranced. "It was paradise, pure satisfaction and excitement all rolled into one," he says. "That's where I discovered what Sheffield is all about. It's about fantastic skills, some of the best in the world. It's about manufacturing knowledge, a depth and breadth of knowledge accumulated over centuries. I became aware for the first time that Sheffield was a powerhouse of converting energy into fine quality products using traditional hand tools and methods of production."

Neil Jagger left school to work at Roberts & Belk – C J Vander one of the world's finest manufacturers of solid silver tableware, hollowware, cutlery and exclusively designed silver and gold dinner services. Over the next 10 years Neil developed his own skills in the manufacture of silverware, and also in

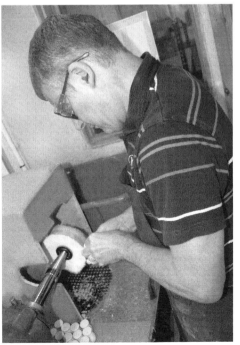

the management of skilled apprentice trained craftsmen. He left the company in 1988, having completed two years as the works manager of a factory employing 90 staff.

He spent the next vital first few months designing his newly formed company's range of handmade shaving accessories and enlisted some of Sheffield's 'mesters', independent silversmiths, buffers and polishers to work to the highest standards using carefully selected materials.

A new company had been founded, with a commitment to quality and generations of craftsmanship combined with the use of selective modern manufacturing methods to create exclusive, contemporary and traditional shaving razors, shaving brushes, soap bowls, shaving sets and travel shaving accessories.

Historically the earliest shaving implements were made from natural materials - shards of flint, scallop shells or splinters of obsidian (volcanic glass) with razor-sharp edges. The Ancient Egyptians developed knives of copper or bronze with which the wealthiest members of society would be shaved, head-to-toe by servants.

Above: *A Present day view of Cavendish works.* **Left:** *Martin O'Leary, 'Traditional Hand Polisher' at Cavendish Works hand finishing shaving brush handles.*

In England, the King historically determined the fashion concerning beards, but shaving was generally the preserve of courtiers and the rich, shaving utensils were expensive and hard to come by. Beards have been in and out of fashion ever since but the manufacturing advances of the Industrial Revolution meant that every man could own a razor. Perhaps the most significant advance in the development of the shaving razor was the Safety Razor developed in the late 1880s and the subsequent King Camp, Gillette's disposable-blade Safety Razor. Further technological developments turned the razor from a single open blade, to a mass produced and inexpensive item accessible to all and the issue of free safety razors to American servicemen during the first world war signaled a worldwide switch from the 'cut-throat open blade razor' to the first razor with a protected blade.

The last razor manufacturer in Sheffield closed in the 1950s. Demand for traditional Sheffield razors declined after the second world war and the old Sheffield tooling eventually became redundant and was scrapped.

Between 1989 and 1993 Edwin Jagger moved from one rented business address to another in and around the Sheffield cutlery quarter, focusing on building its administration and sales facilities, while continuing to sub-contract its production out to Sheffield's self-employed craftsmen. Final warehouse and packaging was still being done in the cellar of the founders terrace house.

During 1989 and 2000 the company continued to develop its reputation for fine and exclusive Edwin Jagger designed products and became one of Europe's leading manufacturers of luxury shaving ranges supplying famous high street brands in London, New York and Tokyo.

Left: *Edwin Jagger imitation ebony cut throat razor. This hollow ground straight (cut throat) razor features a carbon steel blade and features the Edwin Jagger logo on the imitation ebony handle.* **Above right:** *The Edwin Jagger Gillette Mach3 Bulbous razor complete with cone razor stand.* **Below:** *Helen Weston, 'Production Assistant' hand assembling Razors.*

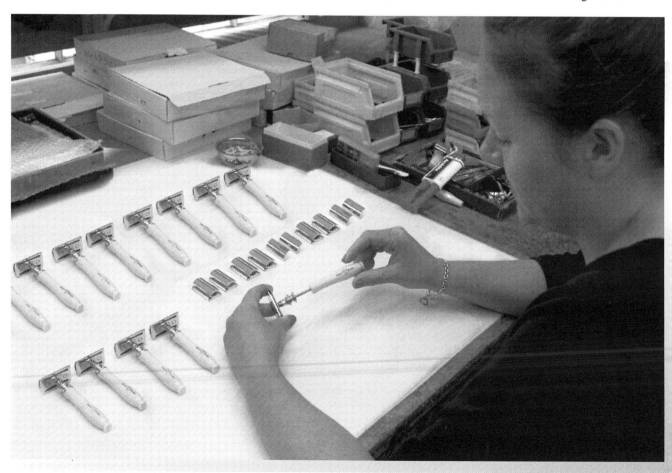

By the late 1990s the company was investing in its own production facilities and in 1997 purchased 7,500 sq ft of dedicated factory space at 6 Morpeth Street and by 2000 had grown to occupy 5,000 sq ft of production workshops, with first floor offices and an increased workforce of skilled craftsmen, warehouse production teams and new administration and sales staff.

In 2001 Neil Jagger began to travel overseas and expanded the company's sales and marketing departments, exporting to Europe, Scandinavia, North America and the Far East.

Edwin Jagger also moved into shaving brush production to extend their range. Badger hair has been used for 300 years to make the best shaving brushes, once only the preserve of the wealthy. Today, badger hair for Edwin Jagger brushes is imported from China, graded according to quality, appearance and softness into Best, Super and Silver-tip categories.

The average brush will contain approximately 14,000 hairs and is made in highly skilled manufacturing process using traditional hand tools.

In 1994 the company rented 800 square feet of dedicated production workshops and employed its first team if highly skilled employees. Two production specialists trained by Neil Jagger in razor assembly skills and warehousing were responsible for the completion of a wide range of razor designs for the expanding Edwin Jagger Limited.

The hair is combed and placed tip-first into a metal forming block with a concave interior to give the distinctive 'dome' shape of the brush. The end of the bundle is tied off securely with strong thread and then glued into a ring. The base or 'shaft' end of the hairs are sheared off (the tips are never cut, they give the brush its desired softness). The clamped bundle is then carefully cemented into the chosen brush handle, creating a luxury that will last for many years.

Top left and left: Techniques passed on through generations are seen here in these images showing shaving brush production. Above right: The contemporary Riva collection, combines cutting edge technology and masterful craftsmanship to produce an exquisite range of shaving tools reflecting a dedication to exclusivity and luxury.

As interest grew in the Edwin Jagger brand the company spent many hours designing and developing razors compatible with the latest razor blade systems manufactured by Gillette. In 2008 the company also recognized a renewed interest in traditional shaving techniques using the Traditional Safety Razor or Double Edge Razor as it is known in the US. In response to growing demand for Sheffield manufactured shaving razors Edwin Jagger commissioned the company's first set of specialised production tools and reintroduced Sheffield manufactured Traditional Safety Razors

Edwin Jagger also has a wonderful selection of shaving creams, shaving soaps and aftershave lotions.

The growing demand for top quality products using only natural ingredients motivated the company to search for something really special. Edwin Jagger's experience in manufacturing shaving hardware gave a unique insight into what is required of the finest shaving creams, soaps and aftershave lotions. The result is a carefully formulated range, which adds a final flourish to the Edwin Jagger brand.

The company understands and shares the environmental and health concerns of customers, and places great emphasis on selecting the very best natural ingredients for its range of traditional hard shaving soaps, premium shaving creams and aftershave lotions.

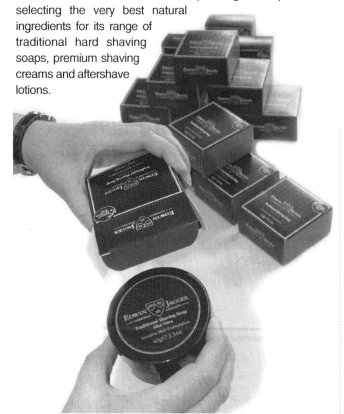

Edwin Jagger lotions, creams and soaps are made from 99% natural components, many derived from organically cultivated plants, replacing synthetic substances and mineral oils.

The luxurious lathering properties of Jagger's shaving creams and soaps are enhanced by subtle natural extracts of Aloe Vera, Sandalwood and Sea Buckthorn for a wonderfully smooth shaving experience.

All Edwin Jagger products are paraben and paraffin free. Wherever possible the natural ingredients are obtained using energy efficient means.

Staff at Edwin Jagger are passionate about protecting the environment and try at all times to reduce, reuse and recycle. Creating beautiful and luxurious products means they feel an duty to deliver them in pristine condition and in smart and exclusive packaging.

Top left: An Edwin Jagger handmade Traditional Safety Razor with hand cut decorative 'Barley' pattern work on the handle. This classic razor was launched in response to growing demand for a very close, smooth quality wet shave. **Left:** The Edwin Jagger range of cream being packaged before dispatch. **Top right:** Edwin Jaggers' exclusive range of skin care products designed to enhance the shaving experience. **Above:** Edwin Jagger 50% recycled branded packaging.

The firm stipulates to suppliers that new packaging should contain a minimum of 50% recycled material. Unwanted packaging is donated to local community organisations and Jagger's workshops and offices re-cycle paper, card, plastic and glass.

From the beginning Edwin Jagger built its reputation on the classic design and manufacture of the finest hand-made shaving accessories. Now successfully recognised worldwide, Edwin Jagger exports products globally to over 25 countries, forging business relationships as far away as the USA, Japan and Australia.

Neil Jagger was and still is the designer of all pieces manufactured by Edwin Jagger Ltd. New methods of production continue to be devised or adapted by him.

The company's international sales continue to grow in booming overseas economies and the expansion of online shopping attracts new clients to luxury shaving items every day.

"Fortunately we are surviving some very challenging economic times by reaching out to new markets" says Neil Jagger. "Ultimately it will be the design and quality of our products manufactured in Sheffield that will determine our success"

Any future development plans will be centred on the company's Sheffield home. "I would aim to stay in the city where it all started," emphasised Neil. "Retaining and developing the skilled workforce we have at Edwin Jagger is central to any expansion plans we make".

Edwin Jagger Ltd is a proud member of the 'Made in Sheffield' organisation and next year will celebrate 25 years of precision craftsmanship still determined to push the boundaries on design and quality to meet the most discerning of customers' needs and expectations.

All around the world people are judged on their appearance, those first impressions matter. Shaving affects how a man looks, feels and how he is perceived. Good quality shaving products make a significant difference.

The firm's desire to create exquisite shaving accessories is as strong today as it was when Neil Jagger began work on his dream in his cellar workshop a quarter of a century ago.

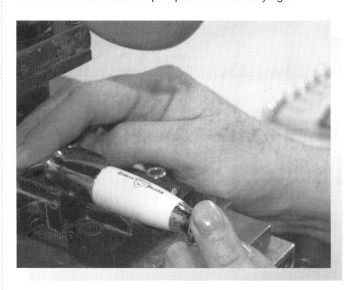

*Top left: Cream and lotion sample packs. **Above:** Edwin Jagger mark being printed as the razor nears its end of production. **Below:** The extensive range of wet shaving accessories.*

Ponsford
A Specialist Company in Sheffield Incorporated in 1898

The Ponsford company is extremely proud of its history and the principles that it has kept to since its small beginnings.

Harry Ponsford had come to live in Sheffield towards the end of the 19th century as a silversmith and had recently married and had a growing family. His silversmithing was his day-time occupation but the local coal merchant asked him to help with obtaining orders from householders on a regular basis. By chance some of the customers asked him to procure various domestic articles and deliver them on his next regular call and this was the very small start of trading on his own account. This slowly escalated into the back room of his small house, becoming a minor stock room, and he eventually found that trading in household goods was more profitable and interesting than silversmithing and this was the start of Ponsford Ltd. He had a pleasant personality and eventually gathered enough together to be able to run a small shop selling household goods. His wife and family helped in the business, which concentrated on domestic goods and at the end of the First World War he was joined by his son Colin.

By 1933 the family business was clearly established but Colin became frustrated as he wanted to sell modern furniture and needed a better position, which matured into the first real furniture shop at 581 London Road. This is the same block that the company occupies today but it took another 12 years before there was another major opportunity to be able to expand on London Road. By this time the war had ended and there were property opportunities and new designs were beginning to

*Top: Ponsfords 581 London Road premises, c1935. **Left:** Founder, Harry Ponsford. **Below:** The growing premises in the 1950s.*

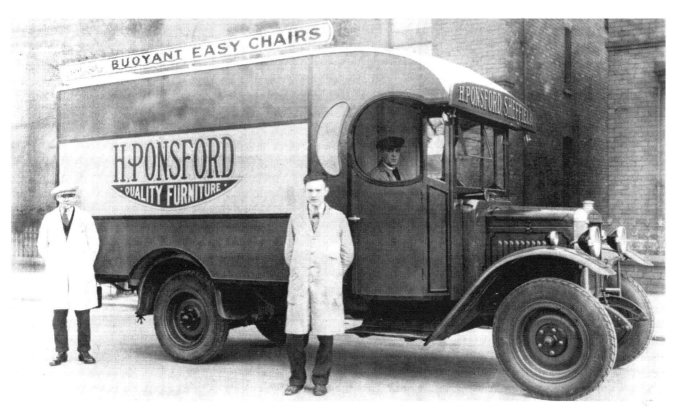

become popular. Colin was joined by other members of the family and all this time the company was being recognised by emerging, leading manufacturers who wanted to sell better quality furniture and better design.

Hard work and growth followed and soon the block of property was becoming a well recognised furniture shop and the company was able to acquire further properties alongside as they became vacant.

Above The first company van. **Below inset** *The main London road entrance in 1958 which was restored in 1992.*
Bottom: *This 1990 picture shows the store running from numbers 579-609 along London Road. This half of the shop showcases classic and traditional style furniture, as well as carpet, curtain and bedroom furniture.*

Its position on London Road was never a major shopping area and the adjoining shopkeepers took the opportunity to move to better regional shopping centres but the site worked well for Ponsfords. When land and buildings behind the store became available, it was able then to preserve the character as the one building and it is now a very fascinating store. This progress really continued to the end of the 20th century and by that time the main block, along with some very good architectural additions, made it quite a spectacular location. By then the Heeley Picture Palace had long been demolished and the site became available for development. This was a major step, but the company took the opportunity to build a new

modern extension called 'The Studio' and joined it with an interesting bridge spanning the side road, together with the improvement to car parks and all the ancillary services that the company would need to progress.

It now occupies about 75,000 square feet and must be one of the largest stores in Yorkshire, serving Sheffield and the towns beyond. It

Top: The sign of quality, one of Ponsfords delivery vehicles. Left: A Marquis Pillow Back Grand Sofa available at Ponsford. Above: Ponsford showroom showcasing a luxury leather Corner Group with recliner.

always had an interest and flair in modern design but this has been boosted by the Studio layout, which is very exciting and coincided with major developments of modern living, flats and major housing

developments that were necessary for the city to expand. Coupled with this is Ponsfords interest and knowledge of traditional interiors and good furniture. The company has always wanted to be sensibly competitive, representing good value, and most customers still want to feel and touch the items that they are thinking of buying, as furniture is a very personal product.

staff in the different spheres of furnishing. Curtains and carpets need careful attention to detail and the company has a good infrastructure for safe delivery and all the necessary storage that is required. Ponsford feel very fortunate to have been able to build this facility which stands them in good stead today.

You will see from the many photographs the different eras of the company's progress, and it is very proud to be able to be included in Nostalgic Memories of Sheffield.

Top left: The extremely comfortable Stressless range available from Ponsford. **Above:** Ponsford Studio Middle Floor. **Left and below:** The impressive Ponsford Jubilee Bridge which joins the older building with the new building, pictured below.

Nowadays, house interiors have advanced considerably with fitted items, more spectacular soft furnishings, carpets, rugs and, again, Ponsford has incorporated these services and the showrooms within the store offer one of the best selections there is anywhere in the country. The company feels it owes its success to its staff who have always been interested in both the product and the needs of the customer. Furniture is an expensive commodity and care and advice needs to be sought as good quality gives more satisfaction. The company now has a highly skilled

Johnson & Allen Never Take a Break

Testing for cracks and flaws in metal components is a pretty important process. None of us wants to ride on a roller coaster or in an aeroplane which might be imperfect.

But how can anyone tell if a piece of metal suffers from a barely visible microscopic crack or flaw caused by fatigue or faulty manufacture?

One way is to hit it with a hammer and listen to the sound it makes – well that's what the railways' famous 'wheeltappers' do. But there are far more sophisticated methods of testing metal artefacts than simply walloping them with a hammer.

Sheffield's Johnson & Allen Ltd has been helping make sure that metal parts are fault free since before the Second World War.

Today's Johnson & Allen Ltd was formally established in 1938. The name comes from an earlier partnership established by Harry Johnson and Allan Allen to make welding rods. Though the partnership foundered when the two failed to get on the trading name has remained to the present day.

Harry Johnson's brother, Lawrence, had been working in engineering and with radios; he had published articles in the Weekly Telegraph as far back as 1922 on how to make 'wireless receiving sets'. Lawrence Johnson had even set up his own radio station from his home in Hind House Lane, a station which featured piano recitals by his wife Muriel!

In 1938 Lawrence Johnson, by then aged 48, took over the Johnson & Allen name and began working from a one-roomed workshop making magnetic crack-detection ink from premises which had earlier been the guardroom at Hillsborough barracks in Langsett Road. The premises were shared with engineers and cutlers Hawksley Stainless Ltd.

Originally the only work done was the production of crack-detecting ink.

The 'oil and whiting' method used in the railway industry in the early 1900s was the first recognised use of the principles of penetrants to detect cracks. The oil and whiting method used an oil solvent for cleaning followed by the application of a whiting or chalk coating, which absorbed oil from the cracks revealing their locations. Soon a dye was added to the liquid. By the

1940s, fluorescent or visible dye was added to the oil used to penetrate test objects.

Lawrence had been inspired to start the business because of the notoriously poor deliveries from existing ink makers. More than sixty years later that early start had developed into Johnson & Allen's substantial liquid consumable business, selling black and fluorescent magnetic inks and white background paints for use in magnetic particle inspection (MPI) as well as red and fluorescent penetrants and developers for dye penetration inspection (DPI). MPI is used for ferrous metals and DPI for non ferrous.

During the Second World War Lawrence worked for the Ministry of Defence acting as a consultant and general problem-solver at Brown Bailey's, where he was given the freedom of the laboratories; there he would meet Harry Brearley, the inventor of stainless steel.

Top, facing page: *Company founder, Lawrence Johnson.* ***Bottom, facing page:*** *One of the firm's vehicles, a Rootes Group "Standard" in 1962.* ***Above:*** *The founder's son, Max Johnson, with a crack detector the firm produced in 1966.* ***Left:*** *An early Johnson & Allen advert.*

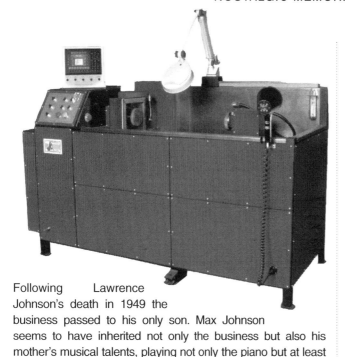

Following Lawrence Johnson's death in 1949 the business passed to his only son. Max Johnson seems to have inherited not only the business but also his mother's musical talents, playing not only the piano but at least nine other instruments as well.

The business moved to its present home in Smithfield in 1950; back then the small purpose-built brick premises and a Dutch barn-style workshop with a corrugated iron roof must have seemed a vast improvement. The first 'bar and billet' crack detector was built there five years later.

The premises were extended in 1962 to make a large single-storey workshop, and then extended again in 1984 to make two further large workshop floors as well as a mezzanine floor for offices. The extra space would allow Johnson & Allen to bring into the Smithfield premises the business of two other firms - VSS Transformers of Portobello Road and FeL Electric - which 'J&A' had been able to buy out.

Max Johnson's two sons, Jonathan and David, both joined the family business after leaving school, both subsequently taking ASNT (American Society of Non Destructive Testing) and City and Guilds courses in NDT (Non Destructive Testing).

Tragically, David Johnson died in 1985 aged only 26; the following year, however, his sister Melanie joined the firm.

By the start of the 21st century, Max (by now an honorary member of the British Institute of Non-Destructive Testing) had retired whilst Jonathan had become Managing Director with sister Melanie his fellow Director.

Jonathan oversees equipment and the technical side whilst Melanie now oversees personnel matters, looking after the company's 26 staff as well as managing liquid consumables,

aerosols, plant and bulk products. Brother and sister also both contribute to the general running of the firm, a business which was by now enjoying an annual turnover of £1.3 million.

Customers for the J&A service would include the RAF, Lucas aerospace, British Airways, the Gulf Air Maintenance company (GAMCO), Rolls Royce and the Oilfield Inspection Service. And it is no longer just inks and dyes which are being produced. The latest crack-finding technology includes programmable automated equipment providing three dimensional magnetic field mapping of components. It's a long way from that former guardroom at Hillsborough barracks.

In 2008, Johnson & Allen became an active member of the AMRC (Advanced Manufacturing Research Centre) The AMRC is an internationally recognised centre of excellence on the outskirts of Sheffield with Sheffield University, Boeing and Rolls Royce being the primary members. It was at this centre that a new company, Vibrant NDT Ltd, was formed. Vibrant NDT Ltd is an Anglo American partnership between Johnson & Allen Ltd and the Vibrant Corporation in Albuquerque New Mexico.

Vibrant uses 'Resonance testing' to screen parts for defects.

Various forms of resonance based testing as used by the railways' wheeltappers have been in use for over 100 years – in essence simply the practice of striking metal components with hammers to check for a 'ringing' sound of the component that indicated a lack of resonance-deadening cracks.

The current state-of-the-art resonance based testing began to take shape in the late 1980s when scientists at Los Alamos National Laboratory began to combine advanced computing power with precision frequency generation technologies to carry out analysis on the

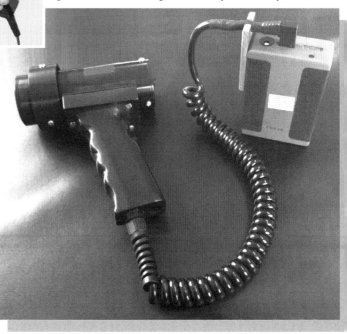

effects of manufacturing variations on the resonance 'signature's of metallic components. This raw but promising technology was licensed by the Quatro Corporation in the early 1990s, and was spun out as a company called Quasar International in 1993. Quasar focused the technology development on the automotive market, spending 10 years and nearly $10 million dollars in the development of a high speed automated NDE system called Process Compensated Resonance Testing.

This addition to Johnson & Allen Ltd's capabilities has certainly moved the company into the 21st Century. Resonance testing is quick, it uses no chemicals and requires only a low power input. It is seen as a green technology where a resonant 'fingerprint' of a component is recorded and compared to 'fingerprints' of known good and defective parts. Pattern recognition software then lets an operator know if the part being inspected is statistically more like a good one or more like a defective one. All this happens within seconds, even on complex parts.

Keeping with a green and R&D theme, the company is always innovating. Johnson & Allen Ltd have been instrumental in promoting UV LED technology to replace old-fashioned mercury vapour lights. The new systems use just a tenth of the power of the old, and contain none of the toxic mercury too. The company

has also developed a miniature magnetic field meter which is the size of a stop watch. Using a miniature TV screen, microprocessor and magnetic sensors the circuit board was compressed so much it is four layers in nature!

By 2012 the company had 33 employees and an annual turnover of more than £2 million.

Having recently finished a huge process line commissioned for Rolls Royce Derby the company now plans to move: another factory below Smithfield (the current base) will almost double the manufacturing capability. With 2013 marking the firm's 75th anniversary in business the directors, brother and sister Jon Johnson and Melanie Robinson, are delighted to take the opportunity to be able to thank current and past employees for making the company what it is today. Jon said: "Don't Take a Break! (Our company motto) refers to our wishes for our customers and their products, and also our commitment to continually move with the times."

Top, facing page: A Johnson & Allen computer controlled machine from 2002. ***Bottom, facing page:*** Johnson & Allen's Neo VU-2 light with battery. ***Above:*** The company's ES-3 Portable Clamp Unit Hardness Tester - suitable for thin sections and small components. ***Below:*** A Johnson & Allen van, 2012.

Atkinson Walker Saw It All

Atkinson Walker (Saws) Ltd, based in Cotton Mill Row, has been making saw blades in Sheffield for nine decades. The firm traces its roots to the former firm of Colver Brothers Ltd, of the Pilot Works. In 1920 Colver Brothers was incorporated with the Neepsend Steel & Tool Corporation, and its saw department was moved in with Slack Sellers & Company. Unhappy with this situation, three employees, Messrs R H and J Walker, and H Tingle left the old company and set up as saw manufacturers as Walker, Son & Tingle in November 1923.

John Walker (the 'Son') had served in the forces during the First World War maintaining the saws and equipment in the Royal Engineers' saw mills in France. He did much of the work when the new firm was established in Wellmeadow Street.

Until the general slump in 1926, the business grew steadily. By 1924, it had outgrown its premises and a move was made to Charlotte Lane. Usefully, the previous tenants, also saw manufacturers, had left behind a well-lit smithing shop and a saw hardening furnace.

Between 1930 and 1933 the annual turnover was lower than in the first years of trading. H Tingle now retired and was bought

out. The business became R H Walker & Son Limited. Having named their premises the 'Falcon Works', the Walkers registered the trade mark Falcon with the Sheffield Cutlers' Company. Falcon would become an established name throughout the saw trade.

Meanwhile, in 1932 Edward Peace & Company, which did Walkers' grinding, came on the market. Walkers bought it and ran it as a separate company until 1940 when it was amalgamated with the parent firm.

The Union Grinding Wheel used by Edward Peace & Company was some distance from the Falcon Works. Saws had to be transported to and from it on a handcart.

In 1937 a site was acquired on Cotton Mill Row for a new, modern factory and offices. Using just half the land, Walkers put up a hardening shop, a machine shop, a smithing shop, a warehouse and two offices. The compact new factory, on the Alma Street end of the site, was close

Top: Richard Henry Walker with his son and grandsons, late 1930s. Left: (L-R) H Tingle, J Walker and R H Walker pictured alongside a 78 inch diameter saw probably destined for a sawmill in Africa. Above: Circular saw toothing.

to the grinding wheel. The new building, like the old, was named the Falcon Works.

John Walker junior had already joined the company when war was declared in 1939. His younger brother, Robert, now also joined the firm. That year, a 'churchill' type rotary magnetic chuck was bought for the new machine shop. It enabled saws to be evenly ground to a thousandth of an inch and also did hollow grinding and bevelling of circular knives.

On the death of R H Walker in 1940, his son John became Chairman and John junior became a director. Later in the war, John Walker bought the controlling interest in Messrs George Atkinson & Company, a Cardiff firm that made band saws.

In 1947, Robert Walker returned from the war and was made a director.

The new grinding wheel was now completed. It was the last of the plans for improvement that had been made when the land in Cotton Mill Row had been first leased, but by 1948 it was apparent that even further extension was necessary. New land was leased south of the grinding wheel and a new smithing shop was built on the foundations of a firewood factory that had stood on the new site. An existing garage was converted into a hardening shop for small circular saws.

Left: A Tempering Goff for circular saws up to 42 inch diameter. Above: Quenching a 48 inch saw blade from the hardening furnace in the 1920s. Below: Sandstone grinding.

Robert Walker joined the Royal Navy in 1942, leaving the two Johns to run the factory. They re-planned the machine shop, motorising each machine. The hardening shop was given a coal-fired tempering furnace with two 42" diameter dies. They made the saws much flatter for smithing and gave greater output because the temperature of the hardening furnace no longer had to be lowered for tempering.

In 1946 work was begun on a new grinding wheel and a small saw grinding shop.

Plans were made to increase the number of products the company sold abroad. However, demand in the home market did not slacken, and it was difficult to supply foreign markets. It was decided to deal mainly in Australia and New Zealand. New Zealand, in particular, wanted the smaller sizes of circular saws which could be almost mass-produced by the new machinery.

John Walker's son-in-law, Bill Perry, who had been a director of the Cardiff firm, now become director in charge of handsaw production until his retirement in 1981. Meanwhile, modernisation continued: gas-fired furnaces, an electrically heated tempering 'goff', automatic toothing machines and the start of injection moulding of handsaw handles with the handle being moulded directly on to the blade.

During 1981 the company introduced the production of tungsten carbide tipped (TCT) saw blades. These were so well received by customers that a major investment programme was required to cope with demand with 75% of output being accounted for by them.

It was also around this time experiments were being carried out to find a substitute for the whale oil used in 'quenching'. A mineral oil was found to be suitable which could be bought from the Anglo American Oil Company at a quarter of the price of whale oil.

Left and top left: Operating the new automatic tipping machine, picture top left. **Bottom left:** part of the new production centre with robot. **Below:** Saw smithing.

In 1950, steel became more plentiful so that it was possible to get up to date with orders. However, a new defence programme at the end of the year meant that soon production was again being held up for lack of steel.

By 1954 it was decided to close the Cardiff factory, consolidating the handsaw and bandsaw manufacturing with the circular saw production in Sheffield. To make room the Sheffield factory was enlarged: the Rifle Tavern on Bower Street was purchased and demolished. The old-fashioned grinding machines, fairly recently put in, now became recognised as a health risk and in any case it was difficult to obtain the sandstones they required. In 1957 the old machines were replaced by a Lumsden vertical spindle segmental grinder with a 36" diameter magnetic chuck. In future, since the demand for larger saws had reduced, it was decided to produce them only to a maximum diameter of 36".

When John and Robert Walker retired, control was taken by Robert's three sons, Chris, Fraser and Andrew. Atkinson and R H Walker now merged to form Atkinson Walker (Saws) Ltd.

During the 1990s export business soared, with sales to over 50 countries, whilst increasing investment led to even higher standards of workmanship.

The Globe Steel Works, and adjacent former cottages in Alma Street, were acquired for expansion in 1991. Restoration of the globe on the building's facia reinstated the Globe Works to its former glory as a prominent local landmark.

Since the turn of the millennium the company has developed a new division to import and distribute saw blades and other tools. The firm has opened new markets all over the world, increasing turnover dramatically.

The company continued manufacturing Tungsten Carbide Tipped circular saw blades for the woodworking and aluminium cutting industries in the UK. It also developed blades used in the oil industry for cutting pipelines, and tines used for aerating turf on sports grounds and golf courses.

In 2006, a decision was made to split the business, separating manufacturing from the import business. Fraser and Andrew Walker formed a new company (AW Tools Ltd.) and moved into the Globe Steel Works.

Chris Walker continued to run Atkinson-Walker (Saws) Ltd in Cotton Mill Row. At the beginning of 2007, he was joined in the business by his wife, Marg, who became a Director.

Atkinson Walker continued to produce all types of circular saws, circular knives, and hand tools.

In June, 2007 in the Sheffield floods, the firm was flooded and was forced to halt production. Many of the machines were unsalvageable. The decision was made to cease the manufacture of hand saws and to concentrate on the production of high quality TCT circular saw blades and other circular products.

Despite the enormous efforts of the workforce to clean the premises, repair and reorganise the machinery, it took two months from the flood to restore production. Although traumatic, the flood gave the company the opportunity to improve its production techniques and upgrade machinery, introducing more automatic machines to increase both efficiency and quality.

Today the company continues to grow. It is established as a premier supplier of TCT saw blades to customers in the UK as well as in Europe, the Middle East, Turkey, Africa and many other countries around the world.

Above: Heat treating a circular saw blade. *Centre:* Surface grinding (top) and laser cutting (left). *Below:* Chris and Marg Walker, 2012

Ancon Building Products
Celebrating 130 Years and Still Going Strong

Ancon Ltd, trading as Ancon Building Products, is one of Sheffield's longest-established businesses. The firm's history dates back to 1882 when George Clark, a great Sheffield industrialist, founded a steel fabrication company. The Ancon name came much later when George Clark (Sheffield) Ltd merged with another Sheffield business, Ancon Stainless Steel Fixings, in 1992 to become Ancon Clark.

Today, Ancon Building Products continues to thrive. It employs 380 people at three UK manufacturing sites and overseas operations in

Austria, Germany, Switzerland, the United Arab Emirates and Australia. The company designs and manufactures a wide range of steel products for the Construction Industry, primarily to support and reinforce masonry and concrete, and supplies a variety of construction sectors including housing, commercial and infrastructure.

Ancon's head office, a 70,000sq.ft purpose-built facility, is still located in Sheffield and actually stands just half a mile from George Clark's former factory at Crescent Steelworks on Warren Street.

Throughout its 130 year history, the values which underpin the company's success have been innovative product design and manufacturing agility. These corporate strengths have ensured

that the business continually adapts to new and varied market demands.

The firm's founding father, George Clark, was born on 15th April, 1857, in Newton-on-Trent, North Lincolnshire. George grew up in the country and worked as a farm-lad. After talking to two steelwork managers who came to Newton to fish, it is said that despite his love of the country he was "fired with a desire to come to Sheffield". From his humble origins George Clark became a well-known and much respected Sheffield figure. He represented Nether Hallam on the City Council for 30 years and was made a magistrate in 1928.

George Clark came to Sheffield in 1875 to work for the Midland Railway Company. It was a good time to work for the railways and an even better time to come and find ones fortune in Sheffield. In 1801 there had been around 60,000 inhabitants, and by 1901, the population had grown to 451,195. This phenomenal growth was founded on steel production, and the manufacture of steel products for which the Victorian age had an insatiable demand.

Above: Founder, George Clark. Below: Staff of George Clark (Sheffield) Ltd pictured alongside their different modes of transportation in the 1920s (Source: www.picturesheffield.com).

By 1882 George had founded his own business in the steel industry. His first products were shovel plates cut from sheet, reflecting his interest in the need to improve farming methods by producing better tools. The demand for sheet, mainly for agricultural tools was so great that by 1908 George Clark had a steel mill at Penistone Road. His business grew rapidly and by 1912 two further mills had been established at Penistone Road: the North British Steelworks and subsequently the Middlewood Rolling Mills.

Always a man given to improving manufacturing techniques and increasing efficiency, George's first patented invention was a revolutionary machine which reduced the amount of scrap produced in the blanking out process.

As well as producing sheet and tools for agricultural purposes the company also supplied the cutlery market. Blanks were produced for table knives, before the company developed its own range in the 1930s. The design was developed and patented by Douglas Clark, George's son.

Company founder George Clark died in 1936, aged 79.

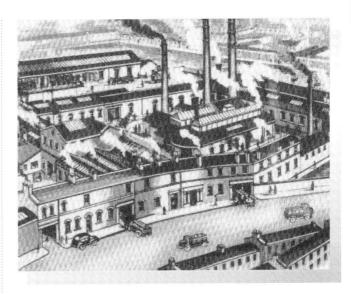

The Clark cutlery, known as 'Voluto', was unique and years ahead of its time. It was manufactured from one piece of stainless steel making it faster and easier to produce, stronger, more aesthetic and more hygienic. In 1935, the company was awarded a medal by the Royal Sanitary Institute. Unfortunately, the 'Voluto' workshops were bombed during the Second World War and the patent was sold, taking the business in a new direction.

The post war years saw many changes at Clarks. As the traditional markets, such as shovel plates began to die away with the development of mechanical earth-moving equipment, new markets were sought.

In the mid-1960s George Clark shared premises with Walter Spencer and Company and in 1972 they briefly merged to form Spencer Clark Metal Industries Ltd. Walter Spencer and Company had occupied a site at Crescent Steelworks on Warren Street since 1901 – an area of land adjacent to the River Don which had seen considerable industrial development during the nineteenth century – and it was here where the company now moved, just around the corner from Ancon's current site at President Way!

The business began to explore new sophisticated stainless steels and superalloy steels, and started to target the Construction Industry; firstly with reinforcing bar before diversifying into cavity wall ties and brickwork support systems. New manufacturing facilities were established in North Wales to service demand. The company developed a very high tensile stainless steel ribbed bar. It became popular both home and abroad, being used to reinforce the walkways around the famous Sydney Opera House.

Left: Clark's Voluto cutlery. **Above:** *Walter Spencer and Company's Crescent Steelworks site.* **Below:** *Reinforcing the walkways around the Sydney Opera House.*

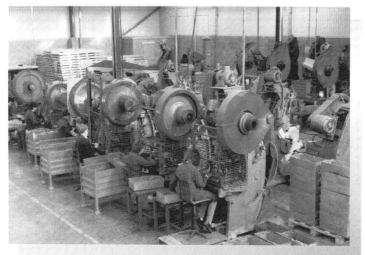

This bar also proved ideal for remedial construction work, particularly on high rise concrete buildings. Amongst the buildings restored using this high strength bar was the Queen's Head public house on Pond Street – the oldest standing building in Sheffield.

At around the same time (1971), on the other side of the city, Ancon Stainless Steel Fixings, was founded. George Clark and Ancon competed head-to-head for some time, with a similar range of products, before merging in 1992 to become Ancon Clark. The company continued to expand both through organic growth, and through a number of mergers and acquisitions. It moved to its current purpose-built facility on President Way in 1997 and has expanded its footprint twice since, taking additional space in adjacent buildings, as well as relocating its factory in Wales to larger premises in Deeside.

New overseas sales operations in Australia and the United Arab Emirates were acquired as a result of a merger in 1997 with Leeds-based CCL Systems. The acquisition of a Swiss business, Plüger & Partner, a fellow expert in working with stainless steels, followed in 1998.

Ancon's Austrian business was founded in 2002, followed by a German subsidiary in 2006. The company continues to expand its international sales network and now has distributors as far afield as USA, South Africa and Russia.

Meanwhile, Ancon's contribution to Sheffield life has not just been industrial. In 1998, Ancon manufactured and donated two 'Salmon of Steel', designed by local artist David Mayne, which mark a stretch of water known as Salmon Pastures on the Five Weirs Walk along the River Don.

In 2004, Ancon donated technical resources and materials to the restoration of Sheffield's iconic Cholera Monument. Built in 1835 to commemorate the 402 Sheffield victims of the great Cholera epidemic of 1832, it had been badly damaged by severe gales and a lightning strike in 1990. Ancon's contribution helped stabilise and preserve the monument for future generations.

Since 2008, Ancon has been recognised as a Business Language Champion for its work with secondary school children in England and Wales. Students visiting Ancon gain an understanding of the essential role that language skills play in today's global business environment – and are encouraged to keep learning beyond secondary education.

Ancon still cuts, welds, forms and punches stainless steel, just like it has for many years: however, the equipment used has changed considerably. Laser cutting and robot welding were introduced in 2000.

Operational Excellence is the driving force behind the efficiency and ongoing improvement of the company's processes.

Top left: A view inside the George Clark factory, circa 1985.
Left: New signage at the Olive Grove Road site after the merger of Ancon Stainless Steel Fixings and George Clark in 1992.
Above: David Mayne's 'Salmon of Steel' manufactured by Ancon for the Five Weirs Walk.

Encompassing the latest Lean Manufacturing and 'Six Sigma' principles, an operational excellence programme helps to continuously improve the quality of products and reduce waste, operating costs and delivery lead times. The everyday implementation of process improvement tools and continuous improvement methods means Ancon is well positioned for sustained growth, keeping it at the forefront of the steel fixings industry.

Ancon continues to develop new products which meet the Construction Industry's sustainability agenda by improving the thermal performance of buildings, eliminating on-site safety concerns and accelerating the rate of construction. The firm uses the properties of steel to its full advantage in order to optimise the use of other construction materials like concrete and insulation, and facilitate more efficient construction processes.

In 2012 on HM The Queen's birthday, Ancon was honoured with a Queen's Award for Enterprise in Innovation. This is considered by many to be the ultimate business accolade. Winning organisations must demonstrate significant advances in commercial success through innovation, combined with the highest levels of corporate excellence. The award confirms that Ancon is one of Britain's most successful businesses with not only a long history but also a very bright future.

THE QUEEN'S AWARDS
FOR ENTERPRISE:
INNOVATION
2012

Top left: *Laser cutting of stainless steel plate.* **Above:** *Ancon directors: Josie Welburn, Stuart Maxwell and Peter McDermott.* **Centre:** *In 2012, Ancon won a prestigious Queen's Award for Innovation for its ground-breaking lockable dowel system used in post-tensioned concrete buildings.* **Below:** *Ancon Head Office, President Way, Sheffield.*

Shepherd Distribution Services
Synonymous with Sheffield's Steel Industry

warehousing facilities offers clients a unique range of nationwide distribution options.

Shepherd's is well known locally for its expertise in the collection, handling and delivery of all manner of awkwardly shaped general engineering and industrial products in small or part-load consignments. Shepherd's deliver more than 2,000 tonnes of this type of goods, made up of some 2,500 collections and deliveries, nationally every week.

The company is also a leading player in the nationwide distribution of 1-3 pallet consignments of all types of consumer goods through its involvement with the Palletline network.

Top left: Rowland James alongside one of the company vehicles in the 1950s. *Below:* The company advertise the new premises in the Sheffield Star in November 1963. *Above:* J. J. Shepherd's premises at Low Road, Oughtibridge, in the mid-1960s.

With a history going back more than six decades Shepherd Distribution Services has built its reputation on offering its customers solutions to their distribution problems. Today, the company's fleet of vehicles and its comprehensive

J. J. Shepherd (Est. 1946) Ltd was formed, as its name implies, in 1946 by Jack Shepherd as a full load steel and refractory industries haulier. The firm was based at Church Street, Oughtibridge. A new Labour Government had been elected only twelve months previously, and with it came the promise of nationalisation of the coal and steel industries alongside the railways. Nationalisation, too, was promised for the road transport industry, but there would still be room for small road hauliers to operate, if they were good enough and tough enough.

Lorry drivers had to be tough. Power steering may have been invented in the 1920s, but neither it nor air-assisted clutches and gear changes were yet to be found amongst the transport fleets of Britain. But if the job was tough Jack Shepherd was more than equal to the challenge. By the 1960s Shepherd's had become one of the largest and most successful hauliers in the area.

In 1963, the company moved to premises on Low Road, Oughtibridge. By now the company was working flat out for the likes of Dunford and Elliot, Brown Bailey Steels, Osbourne Hadfields, W T Flather, and Habershon Steel Strip. The new depot on Low Road was 'state-of-the-art' and included its own four-bay garage workshop and a 25,000 sq ft warehouse.

The opening years of the 1970s, however, were amongst the least prosperous in the 20th century for road transport. Many haulage firms in this period failed to see the end of the decade let alone the 21st century. Most serious was the oil crisis in October 1973 when OPEC decided to simultaneously restrict oil production and raise prices. In a year the price of oil rose almost threefold. Inevitably, the price of petrol and diesel rose in response.

For many businesses, especially those in the transport industry, this was their death knell. Yet Shepherd's weathered the storm.

Company founder Jack Shepherd died in the late 1980s and his son Ray took on the management of the company. At this point in the company's history the fleet consisted of around 35 vehicles, mainly ERF, Albion and Leylands.

During the 1980s, however, the company fell on hard times with the decline in the huge volume of steel which had previously flowed from Sheffield's steel mills.

The Thatcher years saw the coal and steel industries left to sink or swim. Mostly they sank, and alongside them many firms which had relied on them.

Happily Ray Shepherd now saw a new market for the company in the provision of a nationwide delivery service for the local steel stockholders rather than the steel producers. Typically, this involved delivery of not the 20 tonnes of steel for one delivery point as had previously been the case, but several 'part loads' of steel or general engineering products amounting to 20 tonnes in total.

Top left: A Shepherd 60-foot trailer loaded with an 80-foot rail, 1960s. **Above:** A 1983 J. J. Shepherd vehicle. **Left:** Low Road in the 1980s. **Below:** Shepherd's Birley Vale Avenue, mid-1990s.

Three quarters of the firm's fleet of maximum-weight articulated lorries were now replaced by more flexible 4 and 10 tonne vehicles. Overhead cranes were installed in the warehouse at Low Road, and a night loading shift was started.

The new 'groupage' system revolved around vehicles collecting all manner of steel and engineering-related products from the South Yorkshire area during the daytime. These goods were then 'consolidated' back at the Low Road depot where they were loaded overnight on to vehicles for delivery the following day.

The company turned the corner in the second half of the 1980s due to the new strategy, but; even so, more major change was in the offing for the business. In 1991, a management buyout saw the company change hands. Paul Tilley joined the company with a background in business development in the transport industry and he, together with Ian Wood and Trevor Hirst, embarked on the next stage of the company's development.

It soon became clear that the Low Road site was far too small for the company's ambitious plan. In 1993, news came that RDB Freightlines Ltd, Shepherd's main competitor in the groupage market, was going into liquidation. RDB's Sheffield operating base was on Birley Vale Avenue, in Intake, a three and a half acre site which seemed huge compared to Shepherd's base at Low Road. Shepherd's was quoted a sale price for the RDB site in excess of £1 million – far beyond Shepherds' reach. The deal was finally done for £450,000.

The new site consisted of two 30,000 sq ft warehouses, plus extensive office space on the 3.5 acre site. One warehouse was specifically designed for handling long steel products with six overhead cranes, whilst the other

was designed for handling pallets. In an instant, Shepherd's had seen the demise of its main competitor, bought up its vastly more efficient operating base, acquired a significant number of its customers and elevated itself into the big league.

These were heady times indeed for three lads who had just invested every last penny they had

Top left: Full maintenance of the fleet. *Left:* One of Shepherd Distribution Services DAF LF55 18T Curtain Side Vehicle. *Above:* Operating the magnetic crane inside Shepherd's distribution centre.

in a non-too secure transport business during one of the worst industrial climates for years.

In 1995 Shepherd's became a shareholding member of the 'Palletline' network. Palletline is a network of hauliers based throughout the United Kingdom who joined together. Each carrier trunks its customers' pallets to a central hub in Birmingham on a nightly basis and collects pallets for delivery to their own local postcode areas next day. At Shepherd's, quality service is assured from collection to delivery. On receipt of goods into the company's warehouses all consignment are checked in order to ensure absolute correctness. Any discrepancies are notified to customers immediately. From receipt to delivery all goods are traceable at all times, with all vehicles fitted with cab communication systems. Pallet networks were at that time a fairly new phenomenon, largely born out of the needs of an industry generally populated by small hauliers. Small, however, was no longer a word which could be applied to Shepherd's. The company's transport fleet was by now approaching 60 strong, though it was still virtually all flat-beds. By investing in Palletline, Shepherd's had the opportunity to enter markets previously unavailable to it due to its fleet profile: once again, spotting a business opportunity, the company took on a new dimension.

Palletline remains the best and most respected network in the United Kingdom. In 1995, Palletline was handling fewer than 1,000 pallets a night. Today, Palletline is handling up to 14,000 nightly. Shepherd's have become a major contributor to that phenomenal growth.

In August 2010, new co-owners Laurence Abel and Ian Davis acquired the company and the next phase in Shepherd's history began.

Shepherd's has seen its annual sales rise to a figure in excess of £7 million. It has a workforce of 100 supporting fleet resources in excess of 80 and making over 150,000 deliveries each year.

Today, nearly 70 years after it's founding by Jack Shepherd in 1946, his successors have turned the business into an exceptional multi-faceted organisation providing not just distribution services but also storage facilities and other added value services; complimented with an impressive suite of advanced technology modules to support the business; a most remarkable achievement.

*Top: Shepherd's Director Ian Davis (left); taking delivery of a new Volvo FM460 in April 2012. **Left:** The ES400 Motorola PDA carried by the entire Shepherd fleet. **Below:** Part of the impressive Shepherd Distribution Services' Volvo Globetrotter fleet.*

Arkote - At the Sharp End

Arkote Ltd is based in Parkway Rise, just outside the city of Sheffield. Over the past century the company has evolved to become one of the world's leading suppliers of knives to the tobacco industry alongside a range of other products.

Today, Arkote continues to work with the leading machine manufacturers to develop knives which will give greater cutting efficiency and long life at reasonable cost.

The company takes its name from a contraction of the name of its parent firm: A R Heathcote & Company. The original business was formed by Albert Reaney Heathcote in 1881, and was based in Dacre Street in the Park district of Sheffield, where the Parkhill flats would later stand.

Born in the first decade of Queen Victoria's reign, A R Heathcote had previously been a chisel and edge tool manufacturer. The first sale of tobacco knives by him was recorded on 5 April, 1881, to WD & HO Wills for the sum of £24 17 shillings. From that time on the firm would continue to supply specialist knives

to makers of tobacco cutting machines. But such knives were not the only product.

The company was simultaneously selling edge tools, and in addition had a flourishing business in grindstones quarried at Ackworth near Pontefract.

Though the business prospered until the First World War, it soon declined as its founder grew older, and the worldwide economic slump of the 1930s arrived.

Meanwhile, in August 1919, A R Heathcote, then already aged 75, had taken Percy F Osborne into partnership and a limited company was formed. Mr Heathcote was now Chairman and Mr Osborne, who had previously been works manager for J Riley Carr, was Managing Director.

*Top: Samuel Staniforth's circa 1900. **Above:** P F Osborne, known to all as Percy, father of John Osborne.*

Following Mr Heathcote's death in 1941 at the remarkable age of 97, Mr Osborne became the sole owner of the company and assumed the Chairmanship. During the period between the two world wars the company's activities had undergone a significant change. The edge tool business had disappeared and now the main activity was the manufacture of knives for the tobacco industry. The company had also extended its activities into the manufacture of machine knives for the paper, metal-working and woodworking industries.

A new factory had been opened in Sydney Street, Sylvester Gardens, in 1934. P Sidney Osborne joined the company in the same year, followed by John Osborne in 1939.

It had been decided by then to consolidate production and sales by concentrating all activities connected with the tobacco industry at Arkote whilst A R Heathcote took over all the companies' other products.

Arkote moved into its new premises at Hawk Works, Mary Street, in 1962, where it operated as an entirely separate entity from A R Heathcote under the direction of John Osborne and Percy Osborne's grandson, Joe Truelove.

In the course of the Second World War the products of the company were essential to the war effort: in addition to knives the company also manufactured Primer Cap Plates (PCPs) which were used in the manufacture of percussion caps, and tank turret doors which were supplied to Vauxhall Motors. After the war, the company continued to expand and diversify. The demand for its products was such that by 1950 it had become necessary to acquire more manufacturing space. In the meantime there had been a revolutionary change in the method of cutting tobacco: this involved a totally different type of knife being used which in turn meant the need for new machinery and new methods of production. As a consequence, in June 1950 Arkote Ltd was formed. It began operation in Hope Valley and continued there until 1955.

Production was moved back to Sheffield when it became difficult to recruit local labour. There, Arkote produced the modern types of tobacco cutting knives which were still marketed under the old and respected name of Heathcote.

Percy F Osborne died in 1961. Sidney Osborne succeeded him as Chairman of A R Heathcote Ltd whilst John Osborne became Chairman and Managing Director of Arkote Ltd.

Above left: *Sydney Osborne, John Osborne and Joe Truelove.* **Top right and below:** *Arkote's former heat treatment department and automatic polishing department in Hawk Works.*

In 1969, A R Heathcote & Company was sold to Balfour Darwins Limited, after which it had various owners before finally ceasing manufacturing.

Arkote, however, had a happier future. In 1979, Arkote acquired Samuel Staniforth Limited, an old-established Sheffield cutlery forge. As a consequence, for the next two decades Arkote became one of the main manufacturers of trade knives used in the catering and meat industries. That business was sold by Arkote in 1999.

In the meantime, after a very serious fire at the Hawk Works, in 1985, the efforts made by the whole workforce at Arkote to get production restarted illustrated the wonderful corporate spirit of the business. No customers were let down, and indeed very few were even aware how close Arkote had been to disaster. Many of the staff have very long service records and it has been said 'Arkote workers don't leave, they retire'.

In 2002, Chairman John Osborne and Managing Director Joe Truelove took the decision to sell the business and in December 2002 the company was bought by Fi-Tech Inc of Richmond Virginia, in the USA.

Little would change, however: John Osborne remained as a Director until 2007, when Arkote regretfully accepted his decision to resign in order to fully enjoy his retirement. Mr Osborne's contributions to the business are still apparent today.

Fi-Tech is owned by the Bassett family. The company had been the distributor for Arkote products in the USA and Canada since 1980 - although its Chairman Lee Bassett had been involved with the distribution of Arkote products since 1967.

The Fi-Tech company is the supplier of a well known range of Adamantine Grinding Wheels and Discs, first introduced to the tobacco industry in 1967. These electroplated abrasive tools made to original manufacturers' specifications are utilised in all cigarette-makers and tippers, and contain either high quality industrial diamond or Borazon®, a synthetic diamond material manufactured by the General Electric Corporation in the USA.

Fi-Tech Inc. is involved in the supply of capital equipment and spares to the non-woven fabric and synthetic fibre industries. A new company, Fi-Tech Europe, now operates from the Arkote's premises to supply spare parts and machinery to UK and Europe

Meanwhile, close links with special steel technology, and the ability to implement new advances in the manufacturing programme, have been the key factors in the continuing success of the Arkote range of knives.

Yet, although the most modern techniques play an important part in production, the eye and the hand of the craftsman still remain vital in determining the quality of the finished product.

Top left: *The company's former Hawk Works, Mary Street, premises.* **Below:** *The new Arkote premises, Parkway Rise, 2012.*

The present factory, utilising rolled alloy steel and having continuous electric furnaces and automatic grinding and polishing equipment, is a far cry from the early production methods. Strict quality control throughout all processes ensures consistency in size, temper and finish. Arkote products are recognised worldwide for their trouble-free performance and built-in efficiency.

As well as producing knives for primary and secondary cigarette production, the company also offers a range of cigar cutting knives and a re-grinding service for cork cutters. Arkote is also able to supply a complementary range of knife grinding products used both in the primary and making/tipping areas of a tobacco manufacturing facility.

High quality bonded abrasive wheels made to original manufacturers' specifications can be supplied for most model tobacco-cutters. The Diamond Dressers required to dress these wheels are also supplied by Arkote. A world leader in its niche market Arkote, exports up to 90 per cent of its production to over 80 countries. To complement its high quality products Arkote also provides a prompt and reliable delivery service worldwide.

Due to the growth in the business, a decision to move from Hawk Works to larger premises was now taken. New premises were being planned just off the Parkway. The developers, J F Finnegan, were happy to customise one of the new units to Arkote's specification and the move took place in October 2008.

The following year Arkote added another string to its bow. Joseph Pickering Ltd was established in 1824 as a manufacturer of polish. It later moved into the manufacture of boxes for packaging. Arkote was a customer for Pickering's specialist 'stitched' boxes and when the company went into receivership in 2009 Arkote acquired the stitched box part of the company. Arkote now manufactures its own boxes, and also sells boxes to customers who previously bought from Pickerings.

With a history now stretching back over 130 years Arkote is still a thriving and innovating business in the 21st century.

Above pictures: *Views inside the current factory at the box section (top left), cut-off section (above left) and grinding section (top right:).* **Below:** *Arkote's Directors 2012, L-R: Peter Oxspring (Financial Director), Jeff Bassett (Director), Lee Bassett (Chairman), Becky Bassett (Director), Peter Skinner (Managing Director) and Todd Bassett (Director).*

Carrs of Sheffield - Room At the Top Table

The first recorded mention of Sheffield cutlery is in 1340 in the inventory of King Edward III's possessions at the Tower of London. King Edward must have valued the knife as he was very specific about leaving it to a beneficiary in his will.

Chaucer wrote about a Sheffield knife in his 'Reeves Tale' in the 1380s; he can be seen wearing such a knife in the portraits that were painted of him. By the 1580s, Sheffield penknives were being recommended as the first choice for schoolmasters in 'The Writing Schoolmaster'.

The importance of the Sheffield cutlery industry to the country had grown to such a level that an Act of Parliament, in 1624, formed the Company of Cutlers of Hallamshire to provide leadership and organisation to the industry under the watchful gaze of the Master Cutler.

In Sheffield the cutlery trade grew throughout the 17th and early 18th Centuries. It grew even more when new developments in increasing the quality of steel gave the cutlers a finer basic product to work with. Specialisation of tasks also helped the industry to grow. By the mid-19th century, the Sheffield cutlery trade was very large, employing ten thousand people, and by the end of the century more than fifteen thousand. In comparison, London had only one thousand, and then a mere 500 cutlers.

By the last quarter of the 20th century, however, the tabletop industry in Europe was in decline everywhere, not least in Sheffield. Yet, a young Sheffield man named Ron Carr decided to swim against the tide and build a new business from scratch manufacturing silverware.

Today, Carrs of Sheffield (Manufacturing) Ltd based at Holbrook Avenue is the largest such firm in the UK.

Growth from a workshop rented for £2 per week, to a purpose-built state-of-the-art factory of nearly 100,000 sq. ft. plus satellite units and a number of sub-contractors is the result of a three decades' worth of effort and enterprise, a lifetime dedicated to making top class products for a worldwide clientele.

Self-employed, Ron Carr started his business making jewellery in 1976. A year later during the Queen's Silver Jubilee celebrations Carrs of Sheffield was incorporated. The growing company moved into its first industrial premises to allow for expansion of its facilities for the manufacture of silver jewellery and commemorative products.

Encouragingly, the launch of a small range of silver photograph frames in 1979 was very well received within the trade.

Top: Founder, Ron Carr. Left: The growing range of Carr products in the 1990s.

Early tentative steps were taken into the export markets in 1981 through attending the firm's first international trade show. The following year the first major export order was secured. Carrs' flagship product range of silver photograph frames was expanded to meet its increasing popularity within the UK and abroad. The company continued to prosper in the 1980s, concentrating totally on photograph frame production. By 1988 it employed over 100 personnel in several premises totalling over 30,000 sq. ft.

In 1990, a decision was made to set up a silver fabrication department and become self-sufficient in the firm's increasing requirements for silver raw materials. Six acres of land within the boundaries of Sheffield were bought for the development of a purpose-built factory. Progress received official recognition in 1991 when Carrs received the prestigious 'Queens Award For Export Achievement'.

The company relocated to its newly built, 80,000 sq. ft. premises in 1992, and immediately began planning for further product development and expansion. Carrs began manufacturing a comprehensive range of cutlery

patterns and traditional silverware products in 1994: they became immediately successful with customers worldwide. The next year Carrs opened prestigious retail concessions in London's famous Harrods and Selfridges department stores. By 1996 Carrs products could be purchased from the very best stores in over 50 countries around the world.

Millennium celebrations in 2000 gave Carrs a unique opportunity to launch a hugely successful range of commemorative products. In 2002 Carrs won 'The Brand of the Year Award', sponsored by the UK's most influential retail trade journal. To complement the Queen's Golden Jubilee an exquisite limited edition set of 18ct Gold cutlery, marked with the unique Jubilee Hallmark, was introduced.

*Top: A view of the melting shop in the mid-1990s. **Above left:** Each piece of Carrs silver is hallmarked by an Assay Office employee. **Far left:** A Carrs silversmith assembling candlesticks using traditional methods, 1990s. **Left:** The traditional skill of hand chasing pictured in the 1990s.*

and the insistence that every item is individually checked ensures that even in today's world of technology, a craftsman's hand is still needed to deliver the highest quality. The Osborne brand of silverware was re-launched in 2010, with the opening of a second concession within the Silver Room of the Harrods store.

Throughout the first decade of the 21st century the significance of the Carrs cutlery brand continued to grow.

In 2009, Carrs acquired the assets of the Osborne Group of companies, the largest cutlery-blanks manufacturing organisation in Britain. This has given Carrs access to what is believed to be the most comprehensive range of cutlery patterns to be found anywhere in Europe, with an incredible archive of hundreds of cutlery patterns spanning over 300 years. This acquisition made Carrs the largest 'start to finish' manufacturer of cutlery in the UK.

Today, the Carrs range embraces the most comprehensive variety of silverware manufactured in the United Kingdom, backed up by a young design team who ensure that the company stays at the forefront of world style and fashion whilst still reflecting the very best of British traditions and craftsmanship. One of the keys to success has been that of self-sufficiency, so much so that silver is melted, cast and rolled at one end of the factory and emerges at the other as a finished product. Woodworking and cutlery manufacturing divisions, together with the first in-house hallmarking operation, provided by the Sheffield Assay Office, complete a unique self-contained manufacturing facility.

Joshua Osborne first registered as a silversmith in 1709; a silversmith was also a cutler in those days. The Osborne name has had a long presence in the Sheffield cutlery industry, setting its name apart from all rivals. Joshua became Master Cutler in 1724, and from these roots Osborne continues to flourish under the Carrs umbrella. With three centuries of cutlery heritage in Sheffield, the Osborne cutlery collection has a soul and charm all of its own; the retention of the traditional production techniques

Top left: Manufacturing: the Carrs philosophy has always been to encompass new technologies and techniques whilst employing the finest of traditional skills. *Top right:* Craftsmanship in Carrs extensive woodworking, polishing, covering and lining facility. *Above: Carrs Diablo cutlery cabinet. Centre left:* Fabrication: being independent of third party suppliers gives Carrs an unrivalled advantage in terms of quality and delivery management. *Left:* A selection from Carrs Osborne Heritage range.

I resigned, became self employed, and began hand-making items of jewellery. The business flourished as the country planned to celebrate Her Majesty the Queen's Silver Jubilee in 1977 and demanded commemorative silver jewellery and other products in huge volumes. The last thirty-odd years have been hugely rewarding. I was able at the very beginning, to build a small but dedicated team, with the ability and skills to launch the company into a long-term, but ambitious expansion programme, which I hoped, would eventually see Carrs emerge as an internationally recognised brand of silverware and cutlery. I am proud to state that this goal has been successfully achieved."

Carrs now exports to over 60 countries. Those exports represent over 50% of turnover.

As well as The Queen's Award for Export Achievement the company has also won the retail Jewellers Brand Object of the year on a number of occasions.

The prestigious concession in the Silver room at Harrods heads up over 2,500 UK outlets offering everything from a tooth fairy to a top of the range handmade table containing the most elaborate range of sterling silver cutlery that can be imagined.

The Carrs philosophy of matching new technologies and techniques with the finest of traditional hand skills enables the firm both to create a uniqueness of product and maintain the exacting standards of quality, that have always been the hallmark of a Carrs product.

Sadly, Ron Carr passed away in June 2012.

Ron's three sons, Richard, Martin and Andrew, were already actively involved in the management of the business. They have now taken on responsibility for the continued progress and success of the family firm.

From individual requests and commissions to multi-product projects and collections often requiring critical and demanding specifications, a highly skilled development team is able to employ techniques ranging from free-hand concept drawings to sophisticated computer aided detailed design specifications. Carrs has now established a growing reputation for its highly specialised Bespoke Product service, with the facility to visually customise and enhance either existing products, or to create something completely new and unique from a client's brief.

Company founder Ron Carr looked back and reflected: "My interest in working with precious metals grew over time, and in 1976 after reaching the position of production engineer within the same company,

Top left and top right: Carrs Troy House, Holbrook Avenue premises. ***Above:*** A selection of Carrs Diamond Jubilee products. ***Below:*** The next generation, L-R: Richard Carr, Martin Carr and Andrew Carr.

Firth Rixson
Engineering Global Prominence

Firth Rixson, based on Sheffield's Meadowhall Road, is a global leader in providing quality engineered products to high technology industries, primarily aerospace. Today its products can be found in all corners of the aerospace sector, from commercial aircraft and business jets to military aircraft and helicopters, as well as in a wide spectrum of additional markets from power generation to off-highway and Mining explorations. The firm however, traces its origins back nearly two centuries.

It originated with John Brown & Co, a company founded in 1837 on Orchard Street, Sheffield, by Sir John Brown, twice Mayor of Sheffield and twice Master Cutler, moving to Savile Street in 1855. For many years the firm was well known as the largest producer of Bessemer Steel in the world. It was the first company to roll 12" armour plate for warships, with three out of every four Royal Navy Ships eventually featuring the company's armour plate.

In 1908 John Brown & Co jointly set up the Brown-Firth Research Laboratories with Thos Firth & Sons, another principal steelmaking company in Sheffield. Thos Firth & Sons had originally started business on Charlotte Street in 1842 and was renowned for being a world leader in the armaments market, and previous to 1908 had even produced an 80 ton gun. Later, the company moved to the Norfolk Works in Savile Street, adjacent to John Brown & Co. The Gateway Arch to what was the Norfolk Works is now a Sheffield landmark that can be seen in the Lower Don Valley.

It was at the Brown-Firth Research Laboratories that in 1913 Harry Brearley notably discovered Stainless Steel, an alloy that was developed to resist erosion caused by the high temperatures in gun barrels.

After years of working closely together, the two companies innovatively agreed to merge to form Thos Firth & John Brown (otherwise referred to as Firth Brown) in the 30's, which included their subsidiaries, not least Firth Derihon Stampings.

Above: Sir John Brown in the Illustrated London News, 1867. *Left:* The Thos Firth & Sons Gateway Arch in the Lower Don Valley Sheffield. *Bottom left and below:* Early images of High Street, Sheffield and Trafalgar Square, London, with Staybrite Stainless Steel road studs.

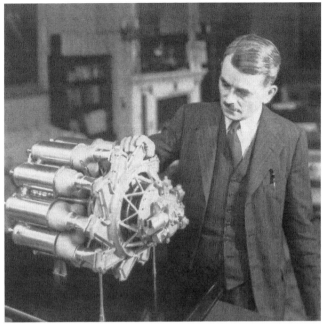

Firth Derihon Stampings produced its first drop forgings in 1919 and consisted of three sites, Tinsley, Dunlop Street and later, Darley Dale. The Darley Dale site was strategically opened during the Second World War as a 'shadow factory' – hidden out of the city of Sheffield, which was then under air attack. The site at Darley Dale is still running today as Firth Rixson Forgings.

Firth Derihon played a part in many major milestones in high technology history, which helped to further promote Sheffield as a leading engineering city. One of the early highlights of Firth Derihon in the 1920s and onwards, was the production of Staybrite Stainless Steel road studs, commonly in use before 'cats eyes' were invented.

The company also became integral in the supply of forgings to the early automotive industry, particularly due to the increasing demand for cars after World War I. In the 1920s, Firth Derihon's forgings were supplied to the 'hypoid gear and axle' that was used on the very first Volvo car, the ÖV4 (nicknamed 'Jakob') and in 1939 the company also supplied drop forgings to the first British designed and produced Ford Anglia, EO4A.

Firth Derihon went on to also become part of the pioneering days of aviation, when the company's forged rotor blades were used on the first jet engine, invented by Sir Frank Whittle. In 1941, the engine powered the first British jet, the Gloster E 28/29 – a momentous occasion for Britain and, of course, for Firth Derihon.

The company continued to demonstrate engineering leadership in the 50s when parts were supplied to the first air-to-air guided weapon, the Fairey Fireflash, and to the first four-wheel drive and anti-braking system car, the Ferguson P99 – a car in which Stirling Moss drove to victory at the Oulton Gold Cup.

Not long after, Firth Derihon also surpassed the competition by producing the largest aircraft forgings ever manufactured, for the engine nacelle of the Bristol Type 188 Supersonic Research aircraft, as well as forged parts for the Olympus 593 engine that powered the iconic Concorde in 1968.

Top left: The first Volvo, ÖV4. ***Above and centre:*** *Frank Whittle, founder of the jet age and the Gloster E 28/29 making its first flight in 1941.* ***Below*** *The Ferguson P99.*

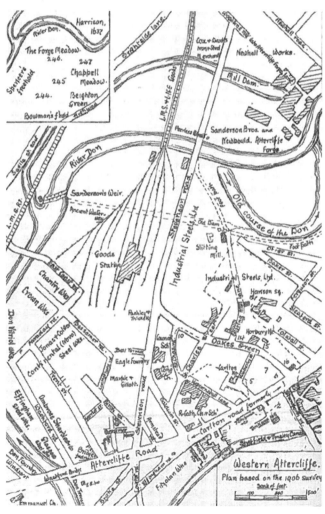

Firth Derihon's parent company, Thos Firth & John Brown, merged in 1973 with the Manchester based company Richard Johnson & Nephew (a company that was founded in 1773). As a result, the company became Johnson & Firth Brown.

Following the merger, the company acquired Glossop Superalloys in 1978, which is now the Glossop site of Firth Rixson Metals. Further changes were seen shortly after in 1982 when an agreement was made for most of the Firth Brown businesses to combine with parts of British Steel and form what is now Sheffield Forgemasters. Other parts of the business, however, remained within the Johnson & Firth Brown group and in 1987 the company acquired Woodhouse & Rixson - another prestigious Sheffield-based forging manufacturer, which dated back to 1881.

Woodhouse & Rixson was based at the Chantry Works, in Attercliffe, Sheffield, with premises in various locations around Sheffield and in the Midlands. The company was well known in the 1970s for ring-rolling and supplying track-driven vehicles such as Main Battle Tanks and Troop Carriers. It later expanded into the supply of rolled rings for jet engine manufacturers such as Rolls Royce and for offshore industries. Reflecting the

acquisition of Woodhouse & Rixson, Johnson & Firth Brown subsequently changed its name to Firth Rixson.

Many acquisitions followed, the first of which was Ring Rolled Products (from British Steel), at the Ickles site, Sheffield Road, Rotherham. This became Firth Rixson Rings and is now part of Firth Rixson Metals. The company then went on to expand its international presence by making acquisitions in New York State (Monroe Forgings) and Nevada (Viking Metallurgical).

Acquisitions continued in 1997 with the purchase of two companies, Barworth Flockton (a family run business in Sheffield since 1881), and Moss & Gamble Brothers, a company that was founded in 1858 and at the time of acquisition was based on Livesey Street.

Top left: Staff Dinner and Dance, Kenwood Hall, Sheffield, 1968. Below left: D. Prescott (MD of Firth Derihon) in front of the Concorde 001 at the 1969 Paris Air Show. Below: A map of old Attercliffe, showing the Woodhouse & Rixson, Chantry Works.

Rolls Royce RB211 engine for the wide bodied aircraft of the 1970s.

River Don Stampings, acquired by Aurora in 1993, also became part of Firth Rixson and now operates as the River Don site of Firth Rixson Forgings. Significant in the history of River Don Stampings was the supply of forgings to the Merlin engine for the eminent Spitfire.

In 2003, Firth Rixson was bought by the private equity firm, The Carlyle Group, and the company merged with Forged Metals, a US based company, further increasing Firth Rixson's ring capabilities internationally. The company continued to expand, acquiring Schlosser Forge Company, California, and investing in new facilities in Suzhou, China, and more recently in Georgia, USA.

Success today and through the years would not have been possible however, without the workforce, whose innovation, dedication and shared vision has established the current company stature. Now privately owned by Oak Hill Capital Partners (a US-based private equity firm), Firth Rixson remains a leader in the supply of products to high technology industries worldwide, with a head office and six operating sites still in the Sheffield region. The company therefore continues to go from strength to strength, investing in further developments and projecting more growth for the years to come.

Firth Rixson - a history of placing Sheffield on the global stage of manufacturing.

A year later, Firth Rixson also acquired two other Sheffield-based companies, T W Pearson and Spartan Sheffield. Over the years the business of these four companies was absorbed into Firth Rixson Metals based at the Barworth Flockton site, Ecclesfield, with the other sites being disposed of.

In 1999, Firth Rixson registered a new facility in Hungary (Firth Rixson Hungaria) to complement the forging capabilities in Sheffield, and establish a European footprint. To further enhance the Sheffield-based capabilities, the company acquired the Aurora group, which included some of the Edgar Allen and Osborn companies.

Edgar Allen had specialised in steel making and engineering, with one of the main sites being the Imperial Works, Tinsley, Sheffield. Those works were closed in 1988 and the business was transferred elsewhere. Interestingly, the site was cleared and was set to become the 'leisure' part of the Meadowhall Shopping Complex (a Tivoli Garden-themed area with amusements and catering services). This was never built and the area is now used as an overspill car park for the shopping complex.

Another Edgar Allen business which was acquired as part of Aurora, was George Turton, Platts & Co (founded in 1882). As it still does today, as the Meadowhall site of Firth Rixson Forgings, George Turton, Platts & Co specialised in supplying to the Earth Moving and Aerospace markets, including the Beardmore Airship engine of the 1930s, the Panavia 'Tornado' combat aircraft in the late 1960s and the

Above: Forged products on the railway at River Don Stampings. *Below:* Deputy Prime Minister, Nick Clegg, meeting Firth Rixson Apprentices, 2012.

GRIPPLE

Innovating from a Welsh field to Global Success from Sheffield!

I f it hadn't been for a Welsh farmer's remark in 1986, 400 million iconic Gripple wire joiners, manufactured in Sheffield, would not have been sold to 3,000 customers in 80 countries; more than 300 people would not be working for the company they own; nor would there be the world's largest 'spider' on a factory wall in the city!

Wire salesman, Hugh Facey, a Yorkshire devotee and an inherent entrepreneur and innovator, could not resist the farmer's challenge that there must be a better way to join fence wires and put his mind to it. After two years in its development, the innovative Gripple – through which wire could be fed, secured and tightened – was 'born' and patented.

In 1991 Gripple Limited was founded and, in the same year, the company's total commitment to innovation was recognised for the first time when Hugh was presented with the Tomorrow's World: Prince of Wales Award for Innovation by the heir to the throne himself!

As business grew more space was essential, so the company, of which Hugh is now its executive chairman, moved into the Old West Gun Works, on Savile Street East, in 1994, following its extensive and sympathetic renovation.

During the 90s, as news of their inventive performance spread, Gripple wire joiners and tensioners popped up increasingly in farms and vineyards around the world, securing fencing and

trellising quickly, easily and safely, with enhancements developed along the way to help customers even more.

The same devotion to innovation and enterprise, which continues to drive Gripple, 'kicked in' a second time in 1998 after the company spotted the potential for its wire grip device to transform the suspension of building services. Since then an escalating and evolving series of systems have emerged from the company, replacing traditional installation methods, with a target of a quarter of sales coming from products less than four years old!

Gripple has a dedicated Ideas and Innovations centre - into which the company pumps five per cent of turnover – inhabited by a free-thinking team of design engineers with a 'can do' attitude towards solving customers' problems with pioneering products.

Even though agricultural business is still essential and growing at Gripple, the majority of revenue now comes from the construction market with products now appearing in places such as the new Wembley Stadium, the Eden Project, the Khalifa building in Dubai, the 'Gherkin' building in London and the Trump Tower in Chicago, as well as to an expanding number of schools, world-renowned stores, supermarkets, 'red sheds' and hotels.

Gripple's core product range of 2,000 items, protected by 300 patents, are bringing safer, cost-efficient, environmental and aesthetic benefits to customers, with exports representing 85 per cent of a turnover which hit £33m in 2011, with a pre-tax profit of £4m.

Top left:, facing page The iconic award-winning Gripple wire joiner and tensioner. *Bottom facing page:* The Prince of Wales officially opens Gripple's Old West Gun Works. *Top and left:* View inside sections of the factory (top) and office space at the Old West Gun Works.

Indeed, national research showed that Gripple was one of 1,000 British SMEs (Small and Medium-Enterprises) which beat the 2010 recession.

A fundamental principle at Gripple is speaking to customers in their native language, wherever they are in the world, with many members of the company's workforce - 100 of them overseas - capable of communicating in numerous major languages.

Gripple also has a sales and manufacturing base in Chicago, an expanding sales office in Obernai, near Strasbourg, manufacturing bases in New Delhi and São Paulo and maintains strong partnerships with distributors and agents across the world.

With entrepreneurial innovation at its heart, in 2004 Gripple spawned a sister company, Loadhog to produce systems which would revolutionise the returnable transit packaging market. Business grew to the point that a Queen's Award was secured in 2009 and a move into The Hog Works, with eight times more space than the company's previous premises, was essential in 2010, and was closely followed by an award as the country's best SME in 2011.

Now with a £7.5m turnover and 50 staff, Loadhog continues to mirror Gripple's 'nothing is impossible' attitude, so watch this space!

Not to be outdone, Gripple's business expansion coincided with Loadhog's pressing need for more space, so the wire joiner manufacturer moved into its second Sheffield factory where more jobs were created to produce the majority of Gripples in the building vacated by Loadhog – now known as Riverside.

Among more than 40 awards, Gripple has been voted the Best SME in the UK by the Institute of Mechanical Engineers; the Best Engineering Plant by Cranfield School of Management and is believed to be the only SME in the UK to have secured a Queen's Award in each of the scheme's three categories – innovation, international trade and sustainability. The company has won a Green Apple Environment Award and a Ruban d'Honneur in the European Business Awards. And in 2012 Gripple won its second Queen's Award for innovation - surprise, surprise!

In the Queen's Diamond Jubilee and Olympics year, Gripple was one of only 40 companies to feature in the Make it in Great Britain exhibition which showcased the country's best manufacturing. In London's Science Museum, the company 'rubbed shoulders' with some of the nation's most accomplished and celebrated companies, including McLaren F1, Airbus, BAE Systems and Coca Cola!

Since 1994 employees have been able to purchase shares in Gripple, a model which has evolved to a point where all employees must purchase at least £1000 in shares within twelve months of joining the company, which believes that share ownership is one of the key

elements in ensuring its long term success by creating a sense of unity and commitment to their work.

With its proud start in Sheffield, where its head office will always be based, Gripple believes strongly that manufacturers should invest heavily in quality machinery and skilled staff delivering a high quality customer service, as well as launching a constant stream of ground-breaking products and supporting apprenticeship and graduate initiatives. Two-thirds of the company's after-tax profits annually are invested in expansion and the rest paid to the employees – the owners of the company - as a dividend.

Although Gripple is synonymous with Sheffield, how many of its residents know that it is Gripple wire joiners that hold together the enormous 'spider' on the wall of the Old West Gun Works?

It has to be said that Gripple and Loadhog are on more than 'nodding terms' with members of the royal family! The Prince of Wales officially opened the Old West Gun Works; the Duke of York did the honours at Loadhog's first building and the Duke of Edinburgh 'cut the ribbon' at The Hog Works! Given Gripple's and Loadhog's ongoing expansion who knows who, when and where will be next?

Top, facing page: The Duke of York and Hugh Facey at the official opening of Loadhog's first home. ***Bottom, facing page:*** The world's largest spider on the wall of The Old West Gun Works. ***Above:*** The Duke of Edinburgh during the cutting of the ribbon ceremony at Loadhog's new home, The Hog Works. ***Below:*** Riverside, Gripple's other Sheffield home.

Hadfield Cawkwell Davidson
Past, Present and Future

Based on Broomgrove Road, Sheffield, the architectural firm of Hadfield Cawkwell Davidson was founded in 1834 by Matthew Hadfield. It now has around 100 professional staff, working on projects throughout the UK. A large percentage of commissions come from existing or returning clients who benefit from the firm's design and management skills.

The firm provides a comprehensive range of services, and enjoys an enviable reputation for the efficient delivery of well-conceived, innovative and sustainable projects, created by design teams with solid experience and fresh thinking. Hadfield Cawkwell Davidson is one of the most modern and forward looking practices in Sheffield. The multi-disciplinary practice includes not only architects but also master planners, interior designers and structural engineers. But, for all its modernity, Hadfield Cawkwell Davidson is also a firm whose roots go deep into the history of Sheffield, a city which this firm, far more than most, has helped to shape.

2012 is a significant date in the history of the practice as it marks the 200th anniversary of the birth of Matthew Ellison Hadfield (1812-1885) who, as a 22-year-old, founded the practice in 1834. Hadfield was the eldest son of Joseph Hadfield, of Lees Hall, Glossop. In 1827, at the age of 15, he entered the offices of his uncle, Michael Ellison, then Agent for the Duke of Norfolk Estates in Sheffield; he was articled for three years in 1831 to Woodhead & Hurst, of Doncaster, and later went to London where he worked with P F Robinson, one of the founder members of the Institute of Architects.

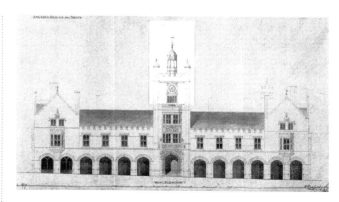

Whilst in London, Matthew assisted Robinson in his design for the new Parliament building in a Tudor Gothic style, even more ornate than the eventual winning design.

The young Matthew's own first commission was to design a memorial to the 402 citizens of Sheffield, amongst them the city's Master Cutler John Blake, who died in the cholera epidemic of 1832. Most of the victims were buried in mass graves in the area still called Cholera Gardens on Norfolk Road.

In 1838, M E Hadfield took John Grey Weightman (1801-1872) into partnership. Weightman had also served his articles with Woodhead & Hurst, but later worked in the offices of Sir Charles Barry (the winning designer of the Houses of Parliament) and Professor C R Cockerell in London.

*Top left: Founder Matthew Ellison Hadfield.
Top right: Corn Exchange Buildings now occupied by Park Square roundabout.* **Centre:** *The Cholera Monument, Sheffield, the first known commission of M E Hadfield.* **Below:** *Design for the Houses of Parliament, 1835.*

The practice was particularly fortunate to be patronised by the Duke of Norfolk. Matthew Hadfield, and later his son Charles, would both work on many of the Duke's Sheffield properties. Like the Duke of Norfolk, Matthew Hadfield was a devout Roman Catholic, and the firm became renowned for its ecclesiastical work, directly contributing to the revival of the Medieval and Gothic architecture in the area. Many noteworthy churches were designed, including St Marie's, in Sheffield, the Catholic Cathedral of St John, in Salford, and All Saints Church, in Glossop.

A considerable number of projects were completed during the expansion of the railways in the 1840s including such well-known Sheffield landmarks as the Wicker Arches and Victoria Station. The Wicker Arches railway viaduct was built in the Roman Style taking the Manchester, Sheffield and Lincolnshire railway for 660 yards across the Don Valley.

The greatest span would be 72 feet over Wicker Road. When completed in 1848, it was claimed that the viaduct contained more masonry than 700 large parish churches - the largest building project in the country at that time.

Victoria Station with its huge 400-ft-long frontage, central entrance hall and two wings, was completed in 1851 and would be a definitive part of the Sheffield scene for more than 120 years.

RIBA, the Royal Institute of British Architects, received its Royal Charter in 1837. Charles Hadfield would become the first Sheffield architect to pass the new RIBA examinations in 1863, becoming the first 'qualified' architect in the city.

In the latter half of the 19th century, the firm was responsible for many buildings designed to house the new commercial and industrial interests. In Sheffield, these included the Norfolk Market Hall (1851), the Royal Victoria Hotel (1862), the Corn Exchange (1881) and Parade Chambers (1883).

Religious and charitable foundations also commissioned buildings such as the Sheffield Royal Hospital (1895) and the Licensed Victuallers Asylum, in Grimethorpe (1875), whilst educational establishments were built as far away as Arundel and Boston Spa.

Partners came and went down the decades. George Goldie was taken into partnership in 1850, young Charles Hadfield in 1864, Arthur R Garland in 1890 and in 1899, Charles Hadfield's own son, Charles Matthew Ellison (C M) Hadfield.

*Above left: The Wicker Arches, now a Sheffield landmark. **Top right:** St Marie's, Sheffield. **Below left and below:** Parade Chambers, High Street, Sheffield, in 1885 (left) and 2012.*

The 20th century saw the introduction of new materials and methods of construction. One of the earliest examples would be the factory designed by C&CM Hadfield for Messrs Joseph Pickering & Sons Ltd, on Moore Street.

Following the death of his father in 1916, C M Hadfield carried on the practice on his own. In 1924, however, Robert Cawkwell was taken into partnership; he designed a number of houses in the Fulwood, Millhouses and Dore districts of Sheffield.

The era of the Hadfield family finally came to a close in 1937 on the retirement of C M Hadfield, one of his last architectural projects being the Church of the Sacred Heart at Hillsborough.

A century after it had begun, the practice had established itself as one of the most progressive of the times, being responsible for such buildings as the Blind Institute, Mappin Street, Firbeck Hall Country Club near Sheffield and for the design of several cinemas, such as the Ritz at Southey Green and the Rex at Intake.

The Second World War in 1939 had a markedly adverse impact on the practice, and for several years afterwards due to building restrictions and shortages of essential materials.

By the time John W Davidson joined the practice in 1946, the partnership was occupying premises on Glossop Road. The work carried out in the early post war years consisted mainly of industrial buildings and housing; a considerable boost was given in the late 1940s, however, by a commission to design a new factory and offices for Richard Bros on Moore Street; at that time it would be the largest building contract to be carried out in Sheffield since the war.

From then the practice would grow to no fewer than seven partners with the breadth of expertise to meet any demand. In 1958, the practice moved to 17 Broomgrove Road.

In 1966, a Structural and Civil Engineering section was created, to function independently as a consultancy service as well as complementing the architectural practice; it

This page: Buildings designed by the practice: the Blind Institute (top left), Sheffield United Gaslight Company offices, Commercial Street, Sheffield (top right) Cairns Chambers (centre) and Richard Bros cutlery factory on Moore Street (below).

soon established itself by successfully handling major engineering works in Sheffield's steel industry most notably at Templeborough, Aldwalk and Don Works.

John Davidson retired in 1974; by then the practice had taken over the adjacent property at 13 Broomgrove Road to house increasing staff numbers.

In the following decades some of the firm's earliest buildings such as the Corn Exchange, Victoria Station and the Royal Hospital were demolished. But those landmarks were to be replaced by new ones designed by the practice. Victoria Quays in the historic canal basin successfully blends modern office development with existing listed buildings. The Riverside Exchange development mixes new housing and office buildings together on a waterfront setting, whilst Sainsbury's in Archer Road and The Moor are just two of over 50 buildings the practice has built or refurbished for that company.

In the new millennium the firm's reputation for excellence won commissions for Liberty Place in Birmingham (2002), Wembley Stadium Concrete Design (2006) and, more locally, Vulcan House for the Home Office (2008), which at the time was the first office development in the city to achieve the highest, BREEAM excellent, standard of environmental performance.

Sadly, the practice's very first commission, the Cholera Monument, was damaged in the hurricane of 1839; the upper part of the shaft was blown down but restored shortly afterwards. Something of its light and graceful appearance was lost when the monument was repaired at the turn of the 19th century when the arches of the flying buttresses at each corner were filled in. However, happily, at the start of the 21st century, Hadfield Cawkwell Davidson would find themselves involved in plans to fully restore this Grade II listed edifice, a piece of architectural heritage which is also a monument to Matthew Ellison Hadfield.

The practice became a limited company on 1 April, 2008, after 174 years trading as a partnership. Today, the modern company unites architects, master planners, interior designers and structural engineers in one practice, combining professional expertise, creativity and commercial awareness. It also unites the past with the present; our history with our future.

This page: More designs from the Hadfield Cawkwell Davidson portfolio: Sainsbury's on London Road, 2007 (top left), Yorkshire Insurance Company offices, 1954 (above left), the Home Office Border Agency, 2008 (above) and restoration of Paradise Square, 1966 (below).

Birkdale School - Actions Not Words

'Res Non Verba' - Actions not words' - is the motto of Birkdale School, founded over a century ago and now located in Oakholme Road. Throughout its history, and today, Birkdale has certainly lived up to its motto.

The school takes its name from its first home, a house called Birkdale in Newbould Lane, Broomhill. Today, Birkdale is an independent day school of around 800 pupils between the ages of 4 and 18, with a co-educational Sixth Form of nearly 200. The Prep School occupies its own purpose-designed site nearby, including a separate wing for the Pre-Prep department. Transfer to the Senior School is at 11.

Birkdale is a highly successful and friendly school providing an outstanding education for boys aged 4-18 and for girls aged 16-18 of all backgrounds. Close attention is paid to the needs of each individual student, developing their abilities, character and confidence to provide the best foundation for a happy and fruitful life.

An exceptionally high standard of pastoral care creates a warm, caring and supportive environment, producing excellent relationships between students and their teachers. A strong Christian ethos permeates the school: students are clear about Birkdale's expectations of them and develop strong values and a sense of responsibility to others.

An enormous range of extra-curricular opportunities in sport, music, drama, academic societies and outdoor pursuits nurture the talents of individual students, help to produce well-rounded young people and enrich the life of the community.

Since its foundation in 1904 by Mr Maurice Asterley, the school's first Headmaster, Birkdale has continued to grow and develop, with expansion most marked in the last twenty years. The school's development and success were acknowledged by the Headmaster's election as a member of the Headmasters' Conference in 1996.

Top left: Birkdale School's crest and motto 'Res Non Verba'. Above: Mr Maurice Asterley, the school's first Headmaster. Below: Birkdale School photograph of 1918. Fourth from the left on the third row from the front and also circled inset is a former pupil who went on to become one of this country's most famous actors, Rex Harrison.

The school moved from its first building in Newbould Lane in 1915 to the Oakholme Building, on Oakholme Road, under the second Headmaster, Mr Griffith's leadership (1909-1939).

At the start of the Second World War in 1939, the school evacuated to Derbyshire at which time Mr John G Roberts, had become the new Headmaster. After the war, Mr Roberts moved his pupils again, this time to Uttoxeter, creating Brocksford Hall School. Twenty boys returned to Oakholme Road under Mr Howard Heeley in 1942 who became Headmaster in 1943.

The Westbury Building was purchased in 1946 from Thomas Cole of Cole Brothers (John Lewis) to allow for the continued expansion of the school. Mr Heeley was followed by Mr John Hall in 1963.

Under Mr Heeley and Mr Hall the school developed to become one of the leading Prep schools in the north for boys aged 5-13, with some 350 pupils and a three-acre campus. The great majority of boys left for boarding school at the age of 13.

In the 1970s there was a growing demand for an independent secondary day school for boys in South Yorkshire; indeed there were two unsuccessful attempts to establish a Sheffield Grammar School. It was surprising that no such school existed; Sheffield was alone in not having an independent boys' day school of the kind available in Nottingham, Manchester, Leeds, Bradford and Wakefield, and virtually every other English town and city of size.

The Endcliffe Building on Endcliffe Crescent was acquired in 1975, it now houses the History and Government and Politics Department.

Now, in response to parental demand, the school expanded to provide education through to age 16 in 1978. Mr Michael Hepworth was appointed Headmaster in 1983. Mr Hepworth himself had been a pupil at the school from the age of five.

Numbers at the school now rose to over 450, and an increasing demand emerged to develop a Sixth Form as parents looked for a school which prepared boys for entrance to university on the basis of a first-class academic education from the pre-prep stage and where a concern for development of the whole person was evident.

Those parents found what they were looking for in September 1988 when the Sixth Form was launched, allowing education through to 18.

The Prep School moved to a new campus in Clarke House, next to the Botanical Gardens in 1988 and now caters for up to 300 boys. The buildings have been totally refurbished to offer up-to-date facilities for teaching.

*Top left: An early pre-prep classroom in Westbury. **Inset left and left:** The old swimming pool which was sited under the current Sports Hall and boxing on the Oakholme lawn in the 1930s. **Above:** Sports day presentations, 1930s.*

Clarke House had been the home of the Osborne family until it was acquired to become the Junior School of King Edward VII School from 1933-1942.

It was then used as a school for nurses until taken over by Birkdale and extensively rebuilt and modernised to provide a marvellous home for boys aged 4-11.

In 1994, the Oakholme campus at the Senior School increased in size by 25% when the Grayson Building was purchased to house a new Sixth Form centre. This building also contains the Language and Classics departments, and new Science Laboratories. The Sixth Form became co-educational in 1995. Further major developments in 1994 included a new School Library and 30=metre Sports Hall. Mr Robert Court took over from Mr Hepworth in 1998 and more developments took place

under his leadership until he retired in July 2010.

The Johnson Building was opened in 1999 to provide new facilities for the English, Maths and Religious Education departments and a base for the Lower School. The Design and Technology Department underwent total refurbishment in 2000 and a new Art Centre was created in the Westbury Building and a Music School developed in Oakholme.

Birkdale has its own playing fields a short distance away. These have been the focus of more recent developments to improve facilities, with a £2 million investment in the recently acquired 125 year lease for the 30 acre Castle Dyke playing fields and the construction of a new state-of-the-art Sports Pavilion, which opened in 2006. In 2012 an ECB approved 10-lane retractable netting system was installed to promote cricket throughout the school. The synthetic surface allows many other sports to use the area outside of the cricket season.

Top left: *Former Headmasters John Hall and Michael Hepworth with ex-pupil Michael Palin in 1992. Famous for his travel writing, Michael Palin credited John Hall's Geography lesson for giving him his taste for travel.* **Left:** *The new entrance of the Prep School on Clarke Drive.* **Top:** *Oakholme, part of the origins of the school.* **Above right:** *Pupils pictured below the Johnson building.* **Below:** *Birkdale's state-of- the-art Sports Pavilion.*

The School has established a firm reputation for academic excellence; virtually all members of the Sixth Form go on to university, with up to 10% every year entering Oxford or Cambridge. Academic standards are high, and the school provides the best possible environment and facilities for teaching and learning for all its pupils. The school's Christian ethos underpins a commitment to pastoral care for each child, a commitment that remains as strong today as in the first year of Birkdale's foundation.

Birkdale attracts pupils from an area bounded by Wakefield, Rotherham, Retford and Matlock. Transport, shared with a nearby girls' school, is available from outlying areas.

All the boys follow a wide range of academically challenging subjects which extend well beyond the National Curriculum requirements. Intellectual curiosity is encouraged at all ages. In the Sixth Form pupils are offered a broad range of subjects to choose from, which is supported by General Studies and Critical Thinking.Small class sizes at GCSE of 20 pupils maximum and in the Sixth Form of 15 pupils, ensure that each pupil has the guidance and encouragement needed to help them achieve their personal best academically. Exam results are amongst the best in the region. In 2011, 71% of all GCSE entries achieved A*or A grade - the best in South Yorkshire. At A Level, 76% of all entries were A* to B grade and nearly a 37% of all entries achieved the new A* Grade. More than half of all the A Level entries were A* or A Grade.

Throughout the history of the school Birkdale has continued to expand, purchasing new buildings and developing its facilities. Indeed, the Prep School is currently increasing its buildings having undergone a refurbishment. For over a hundred years Birkdale has provided an excellent education for boys in Sheffield in the independent sector, and is now the only such school in the area providing such an education for boys aged 4-18 and girls aged 16-18.

Not only in Sheffield is the school providing excellent education: since 2000, Birkdale School has helped raise funds for deprived and needy Nepalese children living in circumstances where education is not an option, as in spite of its natural beauty, Nepal remains one of the poorest of countries. These funds have helped to build the Peace Garden English School, in Kathmandu, which has nearly 300 pupils. Every year pupils from Birkdale have visited the community of Kokhana, a village in the Kathmandu valley. There pupils spend time teaching; it has proved to be a life changing experience for many. About 10 minutes walk from Kokhana is a leprosy colony, home to about 500 families, there Birkdale has also helped build a church and a health centre.

For more than a century 'Actions not words' has been the school motto. Today, under Headmaster Dr Paul Owen, turning words into action remains the school's continuing goal.

Top left: The Sixth Form Grayson building. **Above:** Headmaster, Dr Paul Owen. **Left:** A member of the Sixth Form working with children at Mt Carmel School in Kathmandu, Nepal. **Below:** Dr Paul Owen and Milan Adhakari with eight of the nine Nepalese orphans that Birkdale School support by funding their food, accommodation and education.

SIG - Seizing the Day

The Group's main countries of operation are the UK, France and Germany, which together accounted for 85% of sales in 2011. Within each country there is dedicated divisional management focusing on each market sector. This is critical to the success of the business, ensuring that close attention is given to the specific requirements of the customer in each individual country.

But where has this enormous business sprung from?

The story of SIG begins over half a century ago, in 1956, at the Norfolk Drill Hall. It was there that Ernest Adsetts attended a Telegraph and Star Homes and Trade Exhibition where he and his wife Hilda were to provide the catering. Ernest had been offered a stand for free, but he didn't know what to put on it!

Ernest's son, Norman Adsetts, was at the time working for Fibreglass selling insulation products for the refrigeration of cargo ships. Fibreglass had recently launched an insulation product for domestic use called Cosywrap. Norman suggested to his father that he display it on the stand, which he did, borrowing 29 rolls for display purposes. The catering business had been doing very badly, a financial flop. But Ernest now, by pure chance, had found his true vocation.

Sheffield Insulations Group, or SIG as it is now known, was originally founded by Ernest Adsetts back in 1957 as Sheffield Insulations Ltd. Ernest, together with his son, Norman, who joined the business 9 years later, grew the business into a leading UK distributor of insulation products. The Group was subsequently listed on the London Stock Exchange in 1989.

A born salesman, over ten days at the Drill Hall, Ernest sold, or rather took orders for over a thousand rolls of Cosywrap to be fitted into people's homes. As a result Fibreglass appointed Ernest as an official distributor. From then on the business would never look back.

From humble beginnings, SIG, which still has its HQ in the City on the Sheffield Business Park and UK operations at Hillsborough Works, has grown into a multinational business that generates over £2.7bn of sales and employs over 10,000 people across Europe.

In 1957, the firm's insulation branch was opened in Sheffield and registered as Sheffield Insulations Ltd by Ernest Adsetts. By the early 1960s, the firm had moved from early premises in Ridgeway Road to occupy part of the old Hillsborough Barracks – renamed by SIG the Hillsborough Works. By the mid-1960s, turnover was £500,000; by 1970 it reached £1 million, and in the 1980s would exceed £30 million.

As well as being a leading supplier of insulation and related products, the Group has diversified into other specialist areas of interior fit-out and roofing. In the UK, SIG also installs loft and cavity wall insulation in residential properties through its Energy Management business.

Norman Adsetts joined his father at Sheffield Insulations as a Director in 1966; he became Managing Director in 1970 and later, in 1975, Chairman and MD. Thirteen years later he became company Chairman. In 1988, Norman Adsetts was awarded the OBE.

SIG was listed on the London Stock Exchange as Sheffield Insulations Group in 1989 with 30 insulation distribution branches in the UK. Norman Adsetts was Chairman, Bill Forrester was Managing Director and Frank Prust Finance Director.

The Group's first major acquisition, in 1990, was Ceilings Distribution Ltd, a three-branch supplier of ceiling and related products in the North of England. It was a significant step in strategy to broaden product and customer base within the area of specialised distribution for interior products.

Norman Adsetts became Non-executive Chairman in 1993, and Bill Forrester became Chief Executive. The following year began with the acquisition of the Freeman Group, the second-largest insulations distributor in the UK. It provided SIG with its first entry point into mainland Europe as the Freeman Group included an insulation business in France called Ouest Isol.

Norman Adsetts retired from the Board in 1996 to be replaced by Barrie Cottingham. Entry into the German insulations and interiors market followed with the acquisition of WKT and Golinski (now called WeGo).

Facing page: Ernest's Adsetts and son, Sir Norman Adsetts. Above: Hillsborough Works, where the business first operated from and still SIG's UK head office. Left: Signet House, SIG's Group head office.

Chris Davies took over from David Williams as Chief Executive in 2008. Leslie Van de Walle became SIG's Chairman in 2011.

SIG today is a leading distributor of specialist building products in Europe, with strong positions in its core markets of insulation and energy management, interiors and exteriors. The Group principally operates in 11 countries in Europe and has trading operations in a further six, including countries in the Middle East, serving a wide range of trades in the building and construction markets.

And, in 1997, the Group entered the UK specialist roofing distribution market with the acquisition of Asphaltic Roofing Supplies.

Norman Adsetts was knighted in 1999.

In 2000, the Group entered the ceilings and partitioning market in the Netherlands through its acquisition of Nouwens and UMB.

David Williams took over from Bill Forrester as Chief Executive in 2002. Two years later, in 2004, Les Tench became Chairman.

Between 2006 and 2008 the Group now entered the German roofing market via five small acquisitions. In between, France was penetrated by entering the French roofing market with acquisition of Lariviere.

SIG moved its Group head office from Hillsborough Works to Signet House (Sheffield Business Park) in 2007, while retaining its UK head office at Hillsborough.

The Chairman remains Leslie Van de Walde, CEO is Chris Davies. The Group's main countries of operation are: UK - 41%; France – 22%; Germany – 22%; Poland and Central Europe – 6%; Benelux – 6% and Ireland – 3%. The business has grown from one branch in the UK in 1957 to a position where it is a leading distributor of specialist building products in Europe. In total some 56% of the Group's revenues now come from mainland Europe.

But whilst insulation remains a core part of what the Group does, it has diversified into other areas of specialist distribution: interior fit-out and specialist roofing.

SIG's three business areas are now: Insulation and Energy Management (46% of revenues) - structural, industrial, acoustics, thermal, fire protection, renewables and energy efficiency, fixings & construction accessories. Interior Fit Out (22% of revenues) - dry lining, ceilings, doorsets, partition walls,

*Top left: Loading up in 2005. **Above:** A view inside SIG's Cardiff depot. **Left:** SIG's roofing distribution.*

washrooms, floor coverings. Exteriors (32% of revenues) - pitched and flat roofing products and systems, plastic building products, industrial roofing and cladding.

Since it was first listed on the London Stock Exchange in May 1989 the Group has become a constituent member of the FTSE 250 index. SIG operates from 715 trading sites across the UK and Ireland and mainland Europe, and employs over 10,000 people.

SIG's main focus is on the distribution of specialist products to specialist contracting companies and the professional trades. The Company plays a crucial role in this supply chain. It derives its competitive advantage from taking bulk delivery from the manufacturers, storing product safely and securely, breaking it into specific job quantities that are manageable for specialist contractors. The firm provides an efficient sales channel through which manufacturers can access thousands of specialist contractors.

Using its extensive delivery fleet and geographical coverage to provide immediate availability of product on site and at short-notice, enables contractors to maximise labour efficiency. SIG

also provides its customers with technical advice and product expertise in order to comply with increasingly complex building regulations and help to optimise their costs. Meanwhile, providing credit to customers, and using established and rigorous control procedures, ensures continuity of the supply chain.

Over six decades SIG has grown from an acorn to a mighty oak. And all thanks to a chance circumstance at the Norfolk Drill Hall back in 1956. Yet, chance is not the same as luck. Luck is winning the lottery; chance is an opportunity. Ernest Adsetts was an unusual man, one who given an opportunity seized the day.

Thanks to the entrepreneurial skills of Ernest Adsetts, and his successors, SIG has continued to 'seize the day' down the decades, to become not just a Sheffield business but a business with a global reach. Annual sales now exceed £2,700 million. It is a truly remarkable business.

Above: CEO, Chris Davies (left) and Group Chairman, Leslie Van de Walde, 2012. *Below:* Vehicles from the SIG fleet outside Signet House.

Lincoln Electric - 117 Years of Excellence

L incoln Electric UK began its activities in the UK in 1932. Through growth and acquisitions, it has become one of the market leaders in all aspects of the welding and cutting industry. Through the incorporation of the Welding Rods Group in 1989, Lincoln gained the local expertise in the manufacture of the welding consumables that is now used in the production of Europe's finest MIG welding wire at its Sheffield factory. Lincoln Electric UK now employ over 100 people dedicated to providing the UK welding industry with quality welding and cutting products and services, backed by a high level of technical support.

Lincoln Electric began life in the USA.

In 1895, John C. Lincoln founded the Lincoln Electric Company with a capital investment of $200. The product: electric motors, of his own design. John's younger brother, James, joined the Company as a salesman in 1907. Meanwhile the product line had been expanded to include battery-chargers for electric cars. A welding set was first made by the Lincoln brothers in 1909. In 1911, Lincoln Electric introduced the first variable voltage, single operator, portable welding machine in the world.

In 1914, wishing to concentrate on scientific investigation, John turned the reins of the company over to James who introduced piecework pay and established the Employee Advisory Board, which includes elected representatives from every department and has met every two weeks ever since.

The Lincoln Electric Company of Canada was incorporated to distribute the U.S. made products in 1916. The next year, The Lincoln Electric Welding School was founded. The school has trained more than 100,000 people since its inception.

It was in 1922 that Lincoln Electric's production of welding equipment surpassed that of motors for the first time, making welding the company's primary business.

The following year saw the company give their employees paid holidays, they were among the first in the USA to have this new privilege. The first Lincoln Electric employee stock ownership plan, also one of the first in the country, was initiated in 1925.

While the average Lincoln Electric worker's pay more than doubled during the decade of the Great Depression, electrodes which had sold for 16 cents/lb in 1929 were selling for less than 6 cents/lb by 1942.

In 1936, The James F. Lincoln Arc Welding Foundation was founded as a non-profit educational organisation to advance arc welding as a leading materials joining process. That same year The Lincoln Electric Company Pty. Ltd. was set up in Australia.

World War II brought a dramatic expansion of Lincoln Electric's business, with welded ship hulls creating an enormous new market for arc-welding products. After many Lincoln Electric workers were drafted, the company hired large numbers of women and minority factory workers for the first time. Motor production was suspended to focus resources on supporting the wartime welding product demand.

Lincoln Electric France SA was established in 1953 with the construction of a plant in Rouen, a short trip from Paris.

John C. Lincoln passed away in 1959, his brother James in 1965.

Lincoln Electric entered a new era of professional management in 1972 with the promotions of George E. Willis to President and William Irrgang to Chairman. The Mentor, Ohio, electrode plant was started up in 1977 to produce the company's domestic wire consumables products.

The early 1980s were a time of hardship, with Lincoln Electric's sales dropping 40 percent in response to the combined effects of inflation, sharply higher energy costs, and a national recession. Although guaranteed continuous employment received a severe test, not one Lincoln Electric employee was laid off for lack of work.

In 1986, George E. Willis was named Chairman and Donald F. Hastings became President. Mr. Willis pursued an energetic course of foreign expansion,

Top left, facing page: *The Procedure Handbook of Arc Welding Design, first published in 1933, is today in its 13th edition. More than two million copies of this textbook have been sold.* ***Below:*** *One of the first welding machines manufactured by Lincoln Electric.*

The Admiralty started making welding rods in Sheffield in the 1920s. When war broke out in 1939 it wanted to increase output so asked Harry Brearley for help. He had set up a welding rod manufacturing section within Brown Bayleys in 1932. After the war the welding rod manufacturing division was privatised, still with Brearley as Technical Director, to become Welding Rods Ltd.

In 1986, Welding Rods Ltd became part of the European Norweld Welding Group operating from ten wholly owned regional offices nationwide trading as Weldro Welding Supplies. In 1991 Lincoln Electric acquired the Norweld Group. This acquisition led to the merger in the UK of Welding Rods and Big 3 Lincoln, firstly as Lincoln Weldro and later Lincoln Electric UK Limited.

A major refurbishment of the Mansfield Road site was undertaken in 1992 with new warehousing and offices comprising of over 4,000 square metres.

As a result of the continuing decline in UK and European shipbuilding (the major customer segment) the decision to cease manufacturing at the Aston site brought to an end over 60 years of electrode manufacture in Sheffield.

By this time the MIG welding process had started to replace the traditional stick welding particularly in production shop environments, Lincoln Electric built a new 5000 square metres manufacturing plant in the heart of the old steel production area of Sheffield, the Don Valley. Based in Attercliffe this factory today produces premium solid MIG welding wires under the SupraMIG brand name.

ISO9001 was acquired in 1998, along with further investment of £1,000,000 in new equipment to meet the growing demand for MIG wire products both from the UK and Europe

The year 2000 saw the introduction of a new automated packaging line. 2002-2004 saw further capital investment in the factory, equating to £1million. 2004 witnessed the best production year since the opening of the factory with over 12,000 tonnes of premium MIG wire produced.

In 2005, the firm became one of the first companies within the welding industry to achieve the ISO14001 accreditation.

The following year saw the introduction of the manufacture of submerged arc welding wires in the Sheffield plant. This was also a new record year for production which saw volumes reaching 13,000 tonnes.

A phased programme of equipment replacement was completed in 2011; the total investment exceeding £5m.

The productivity trend over the last 10 years has seen a gradual increase - partly as a result of new equipment, partly as a result of better working practices.

Sheffield consistently achieves one of the highest productivity figures of Lincoln Electric's solid wire manufacturing plants located around the world. An investment in new equipment has facilitated reduction of almost 50% in the kWh of electricity per tonne of wire produced. Given that it spends as much on electricity as it does on direct labour, this has major cost implications as well as environmental ones.

John M. Stropki was named Chairman, President and Chief Executive Officer, becoming only the seventh Chairman in the Company's history.

Lincoln Electric acquired J.W. Harris Co., a global leader in brazing and soldering alloys, in 2005.

The acquisition of Metrode Products Limited in 2006, a UK-based manufacturer of nickel-based cored wire and stick electrode consumables, expanded the Company's offering of specialty consumables for the process and power generation industries.

In 2007, Lincoln Electric invested in expanding its global manufacturing footprint, the largest undertaking in its history, constructing or upgrading ten plants throughout the world.

Acquiring Vernon Tool Company, a manufacturer of computer-controlled pipe cutting equipment, expanded Lincoln's automation solutions, while acquisitions in China and Poland further enhanced the Company's global market position.

The acquisition of Brastak in Brazil expanded the Company's offering of brazing products and its Electro-Arco acquisition in Portugal added to its manufacturing capacity in Europe.

Lincoln Electric introduced 108 new products within a nine-month period in 2009, including the VRTEX™ 360, a virtual welding training system.

The Company also opened a 100,000-square-foot welding consumables facility in Chennai, India, to serve growing demand in the Asia Pacific region. Lincoln Electric also acquired full ownership of Jinzhou Jin Tai Welding and Metal Co. to expand its manufacturing capacity in China, the fastest growing welding market in the world.

When the Company celebrated its 115th anniversary in 2010 it became the subject of the book 'Spark', written by Canadian economics journalist Frank Koller. The book recognised Lincoln Electric for its rich history, strong culture and fundamental principles that have persisted down the years.

Meanwhile, in Britain, 2011 saw the return of the Worldskills finals, the World's largest Skills event to the UK, for the first time in over 25 years. This event was held in London in October 2011; Lincoln Electric was one of the main sponsors with its product being used in no less than seven skills areas.

Today Lincoln Electric are the largest manufacturer of welding products in the UK and with the recent acquisition of Weartech now boasts three manufacturing locations, supporting a broad cross section of customers for whom welding is an important part of their manufacturing process.

Lincoln Electric's enduring passion for the development and application of welding technologies will continue to drive them to develop and create total solutions that assist their customers to be more productive and successful in the future.

Top left, facing page: **Lincoln Electric's factory. Bottom, facing page:** *A selection of Lincoln Electric products.* **Above:** *Business Secretary, Vince Cable, is given a demonstration at the 2011 Worldskills final.* **Below:** *The Lincoln Electric head office.*

G & M Lunt
A Final Service

Bereavement is always a difficult time for families. It is a time when people are often confused and distressed; a time when a helping hand from someone who knows what to do is most needed, and is most welcome.

It was out of this universal need, one common to all people and cultures throughout history, that there arose the profession of undertaker.

The professional undertaker today, however, is far removed from those persons who might have taken on that role a century ago – or even less. For ordinary folk before the Great War it was very often a local woman, often also the local midwife, who might be given the task of laying out the departed. A coffin might well be commissioned simply from the local joiner. As for a chapel of rest – very likely that would just be the front room – and for those who had no front room then the kitchen, perhaps the only room they had.

Undertakers did exist of course, but there were simply far fewer of them. But times moved on; many of the joiners who made

coffins branched out to become fully fledged undertakers, the source of many of today's firms. Meanwhile, other firms began to emerge from along other professional routes, such as taxi proprietors, as the need and demand for better quality funeral services became apparent as the twentieth century progressed.

One such firm is that of G & M Lunt now based in Camping Lane, Sheffield.

The Lunt funeral home is family run, independent and, as member of the National Association of Funeral Directors, the firm adheres to a strict code of practice.

Every funeral provided by Lunts is a most personal occasion, and therefore staff feel it is important to reflect every bereaved family's particular requirements and circumstances in each individual service.

Staff offer a sympathetic service, discreetly efficient, and at the same time competitively priced. Funeral arrangements can be made either at the firm's funeral home or alternatively in the comfort or clients' own homes.

The origins of G & M Lunt go back many decades to the 1920s.

Shortly after the First World War and at the age of 24, George Lunt was demobbed from Norton Aerodrome where he had been serving in the Royal Flying Corps, he returned to the family home together with his long time sweetheart and wife of just one year, Mabel Evans. Using some of the skills he acquired during his time serving his country, George started up his own motorcycle repair workshop on Tyzack Road, Woodseats.

It was in 1932 that George eventually made the decision that undertaking was to be his future. George and Mabel began trading as G & M Lunt funeral directors from their home on Meadowhead.

Top, facing page: *Founder, George Lunt.* **Bottom, facing page:** *George in the 1920s outside 20 Meadowhead.* **Above:** *A police inspector's funeral approaching Abbey Lane Cemetery in the 1930s.* **Below:** *1950s Austin Sheerline fleet outside G & M Lunt.*

In the late 1920s, George and Mabel bought their own house at the bottom of Meadowhead. While they were here, George bought himself a car and used it as a taxi to bring in extra income. During this time, George was approached by several of the region's funeral directors asking him to drive his taxi to carry mourners to and from the funeral service, George also acting as a Pall Bearer on many occasions. He found he enjoyed the work, especially the opportunity to help bereaved families, and this gave him food for thought about a total career change.

George wanted to give the local community a complete funeral service. Taking the best things he had learned from those he worked for, he had a vision of how he wanted to improve what was already on offer.

However, the 1930s were not an auspicious decade to begin any new enterprise. Not for nothing was the period known as 'The Hungry Thirties'. The Wall Street Crash of 1929 had brought down the post war prosperity of the 'Roaring Twenties'. In Britain millions were unemployed and thousands of children got used to going to school without any breakfast. Far from new businesses being a success the story, almost everywhere, in every newspaper, was rather one of existing businesses going bust.

Yet, there is always room at the top. The best will always survive, indeed thrive, even in a recession.

In Sheffield the Lunts' business developed quickly, with G & M Lunt gaining a well-earned reputation for a quality, caring and respectful service to clients. It soon became obvious that their Meadowhead home was not large enough for the business to grow. This led to the purchase of the current premises at 1-13 Camping Lane, on the corner of Abbey Lane, Woodseats. The building itself required a total refurbishment and also the addition of garage space and a coffin workshop area, with George doing a lot of the work himself.

With their children getting older and able to help out more G & M Lunt went from strength to strength. As soon as he able to, George and Mabel's son Jack joined the business full time. The work came naturally to him as he had grown up learning from his father all the time. The next couple of years saw their other three children, Mary, Austin and Joan, join the staff in various positions in what had now become a real family firm.

The following decades saw G & M Lunt grow and grow. In 1974, George Lunt was honoured to be presented with the 'Benemerenti Medal' bestowed on him by Pope Paul IV; this was in recognition of his work and generosity to the Roman Catholic Church. In 1947, George Lunt had presented the church of Our Lady and St Thomas, Meadowhead, with a pipe organ. It has been said that this instrument originated from the 17th Century parish church in the village of Ashopton that was flooded in the 1930s to create the Ladybower Reservoir. George had acquired the organ from the doomed church in Ashopton and had stored it in Sheffield until the end of the Second World War.

In the last few years Michael and Andrew have overseen an extensive building improvement programme, which included an extension and the addition of a service chapel to the premises, whilst also upgrading the vehicles to a brand new fleet of Volvo hearses and limousines. The families the firm serves experience all the modern comforts, whilst the firm still also retains the old fashioned, traditional values and service that encapsulate the high standards George and Mabel Lunt first envisaged being able to provide to the bereaved over 80 years ago.

To this day, the name G & M Lunt is synonymous with Catholics in Sheffield, carrying out funerals for many of the clergy, including in 1996, the Bishop Emeritus of Hallam, Gerald Moverley, at which crowds of mourners lined the cortege route.

During 1969, following a spell in the Sheffield and Rotherham constabulary, Jack's son, and the firm's current owner, Michael, joined the firm as a funeral director's assistant; this assistant's role was in order to give him a complete knowledge and understanding of all the different elements and responsibilities that go into putting a bespoke funeral service together. Michael was lucky that he got excellent tutelage from both his father and grandfather, this allowed the original tradition and etiquette to be passed on to the third generation. Mary's son, Andrew, soon followed down the same path, picking up all the skills required.

Sadly, George passed away in 1976, this left the day-to-day running of the business to Jack, who continued to expand   G & M Lunt for the next 11 years until his own death in 1987.

It was now George Lunt's two grandsons, Michael and Andrew, who had control of the family business. The extensive experience and knowledge of undertaking that they had already gained allowed them to develop the firm even further.

Michael, in particular, has been in the industry for over 40 years and admits he has seen many changes to people's attitude towards death and funerals. In recent years he has noted that more and more people choose to have a funeral service based on the life of their loved ones, rather than a religious service, as they did more often than not in days gone by. He has also noticed a large rise in the number of people willing to plan and pay for their own funerals in advance; with this in mind G & M Lunt now work in association with Funeral Planning Services to offer an outstanding and competitively priced pre-paid plan.

Top, facing page: George's son, Jack, pictured in the late 1960s. *Bottom, facing page:* G & M Lunt's 1-13 Camping Lane premises. *Above:* Part of the G & M Lunt Volvo fleet. *Below:* George Michael Lunt and Staff, 2012.

JRI Orthopaedics
Innovation in Practice

JRI Orthopaedics Ltd is a Sheffield-based manufacturer of orthopaedic implants and surgical instrumentation. Company administration and finance are based in a London office. Manufacturing is based in a modern Sheffield facility in Churchill Way, Chapeltown, alongside Research, Product Development, Customer Service, Marketing, Warehousing and Distribution.

The company is renowned for the innovation of the Furlong® Hydroxyapatite Ceramic (H-A.C) Coated Total Hip Replacement (THR), which was the first H-A.C Coated THR in the world. The Furlong® H-A.C Coated THR has achieved clinical success globally. New products are continuing to be developed and introduced.

For the whole of human history, until fifty or so years ago, those whose hip joints failed were condemned to spend the remainder of their lives as cripples. Accident, wear and tear, and disease, led to millions becoming first reliant upon walking sticks, then, as their problems worsened, becoming housebound. Today, thanks to pioneering surgeons, lives have been transformed.

Since JRI first introduced the Furlong total hip replacement in 1985 it has been implanted in over 200,000 patients worldwide. The well documented long term results demonstrate that it is one of the safest and most clinically successful hip replacements available today.

The company was founded in 1970 by eminent surgeon Mr Ronald Furlong FRCS. Ronald Furlong was a leading hip replacement surgeon whose worries about the artificial hip prostheses used by other orthopaedic surgeons led him to design his own - the Furlong Straight Stem - with which Queen Elizabeth the Queen Mother would be fitted.

The son of a businessman, Ronald John Furlong was born at Woolwich in 1909, and went to Eltham College. He qualified in 1931 at St Thomas's Hospital, where he was to spend much of his working life. Awarded the Cheselden Medal in Anatomy and Surgery in 1932, Ronald quickly established himself as a high-flier; he passed his exams for Fellowship of the Royal College of Surgeons at 25, though he had to wait three more years before he could add FRCS to his name.

On the outbreak of war in 1939 Ronald was at the Rowley Bristow Hospital in Surrey, from where he joined the Royal Army Medical Corps. In the course of being posted to North Africa, Egypt and Italy as Officer in Charge, No 2 General Hospital, he demonstrated a prodigious work ethic: while at

*Top: Founder, Ronald Furlong. **Left:** Mr & Mrs Furlong and HRH The Princess Royal arrive at the official opening of the new H.A Coating Plant in 1997. **Above:** Guests receive a demonstration at JRI Manufacturing.*

Caserta in Italy for example he treated some two hundred broken thigh bones. It was his work amongst the civilian population of Milan, which led to Ronald also becoming adept at treating hand injuries, the work earned him a special blessing from Pope Pius XII. An event key to his subsequent career, however, came in a German hospital. Inspecting patients there, he noticed an unusual implant in a German soldier, a 'Küntscher nail'. The 'nail'

was an internal fixation device used to maintain the position of the fracture fragments in the long bones of the arms and legs during healing; it had been invented by German surgeon Gerhard Küntscher in 1939, and was first used in the German military in 1942.

When the war came to a close in 1945 the War Department instructed Ronald to seek the origins of the Küntscher nail - which he did by first tracking down a professor hiding in Vienna who directed him to Dr Küntscher himself in Kiel. Ronald brought the novel medical device to the Millbank Military Hospital in London, from where it was handed it over to a British surgical manufacturer. The result was that it remained in production for more than half a century. Meanwhile, without asking him, St Thomas's appointed Ronald to a consultantship. The hospital sent him to study under the leading orthopaedic surgeons of America and Europe.

Tall, well-built and with striking looks, he was both a fine teacher and a fine performer. In 1946 one of his students

recorded in his diary seeing Ronald back at the hospital: "As usual, the outpatient department was invaded by the orthopaedic surgeons. We had 'RF' in uniform, back from Italy, to teach us. And although he was as full of mannerisms as them all, he taught well.

Ronald Furlong was one of that long-gone generation of larger-than-life, pre-war, pre-NHS hospital consultants, like Sir Lancelot Spratt caricaturised in Richard Gordon's novel 'Doctor in the House'. He was said to be passionate and determined, and once he had taken up an idea he would never let it drop. He was fond of quoting Machiavelli's remark that 'the innovator has for enemies all those who have done well under the old conditions'. Sometimes seeing people as being either with him or against him, he once threatened to sue a surgical colleague who commented that something he had said was unsupported by evidence.

Yet, if Ronald had some weaknesses his strengths far outweighed them.

He found time to study biomechanics under Professor Friedrich Pauwels at Aachen, Germany, having first taken German lessons at the Berlitz school in London early each morning.

Above: The JRI team in 1988. Below: Management and staff pictured on the site of JRI's new 18 Churchill Way premises prior to construction.

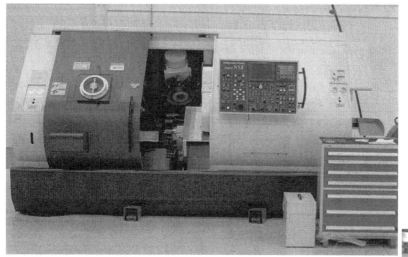

Sheffield, to produce not only artificial hips but also the surgical instruments surgeons needed to fit them.

The first prosthesis cast for JRI was made at CCA, Centaur Cast Alloys, of Sheffield and was machine finished by Downs Surgical in the city.

JRI (Manufacturing) Ltd was inaugurated in Sheffield in 1977, at first with just one man, and one finishing machine, which he made himself.

He subsequently translated into English Pauwels's books: his 'Atlas of the biomechanics of the normal and diseased hip' (1978) and 'Biomechanics of the locomotor apparatus' (1980), as well as Braun and Fischer's 'On the Centre of Gravity of the Human Body' (1986). He was one of only five holders of the Pauwels Medal for Biomechanics. By then, Ronald's name had long become synonymous with hip replacement surgery and with the associated prostheses.

It was in the late 1960s that hip replacement surgery was introduced to Britain. Its pioneer was Manchester-based Sir John Charnley. But instead of using Charnley's prostheses manufactured in Leeds, Ronald Furlong started importing a Swiss variation, the Muller hip, for his patients at St Thomas's Hospital, London. When there were difficulties in importing the Muller hip, Ronald set up his own company to both order and distribute them.

Ronald Furlong retired from his post at St Thomas's in 1974, though he continued in private practice at the Queen Victoria Hospital at East Grinstead, West Sussex. From there he set up a second company, this time in

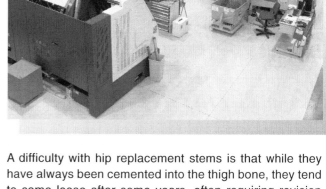

A difficulty with hip replacement stems is that while they have always been cemented into the thigh bone, they tend to come loose after some years, often requiring revision surgery. In response cementless prostheses were therefore developed.

Ronald Furlong and Professor Johannes Osborn of Bonn developed a cementless prosthesis in the 1980s. The new prosthesis aimed to be totally compatible with bone and consisted of the mineral hydroxy-apatite which was then coated onto the shaft of the artificial joint.

In 1985, Ronald implanted the first of the new artificial joints in a patient. The apatite-coated prosthesis won a 1993 Queen's Award for Technological Achievement:

*Top left and top right: Modern state-of-the-art machinery inside JRI's new Churchill Way facility. **Left, far left and above right**: Manufacturing the JRI hip joint, pictured above right.*

In 2007, JRI moved from its premises in Leigh Street, Attercliffe Common, to new 5,300 sqm, state-of-the-art premises in Churchill Way, Chapeltown. The £6 million investment showed just how far JRI had grown in three decades.

Ronald Furlong retained his energy and skills into old age, performing his last operation only five years before his death, aged 93 in 2002. With his wife Eileen he used to spend the summer months in Switzerland, where he died of heart failure after a short illness.

Queen Elizabeth the Queen Mother was fitted with a cemented Furlong Straight Stem in 1995 and again in 1998. In 1989, Ronald Furlong inaugurated a charity, the Furlong Research Foundation, to evaluate the efficacy of his coated prostheses over the long-term.

Following the death of Eileen Furlong in 2003, ownership of JRI was given to the Foundation – the registered charity which the Furlongs had set up in 1989 to support medical education and research in orthopaedics. The continued development and commercial success of JRI allows the company to Gift Aid a significant proportion of profits to the Foundation.

Today, led by Chairman Brian Jones and Managing Director Keith Jackson, JRI continues to innovate and develop products which enhance the lives of thousands upon thousands of people all around the world.

*Top left: Visitors and dignitaries including the Mayor and Mayoress of Sheffield are given a tour of the new facility. **Left and below:** Managing Director Keith Jackson welcomes Ex-England fast bowler Darren Gough to officially open the new JRI premises pictured below, 2007. **Right:** Chairman, Brian Jones.*

When the Max Rayne Foundation gave £750,000 to St Thomas's in 1994, and shortly afterwards its founder, Max Rayne, broke a vertebra in a boating accident at Cannes, Ronald was flown out to see him.

Ronseal®

Does exactly what it says on the tin®

IT'S one of the UK's best-known brands - and does exactly what it says on the tin. The eye-catching advertising slogan, favoured by politicians, presenters and pop stars, was coined by an ad agency engaged by Ronseal and has become one of the buzz phrases of the decade.

"It just seemed to capture the public imagination," explains Ronseal's marketing manager Kate Sitch. "Millions of do-it-yourself enthusiasts using our products were familiar with their quality and durability but the campaign, beamed into homes across the country, gained a whole new audience for Ronseal. Now rarely a day goes by without hearing the phrase on someone's lips."

But there's more to the woodcare products manufacturer than innovative advertising. The company has a chequered history going back well over 100 years. Throughout that time it has remained alert to changing styles and demands, pioneering new products to meet them. Ownership may have changed but the company's commitment to researching and developing new and improved products has been consistent. From T.M. Fowler manufacturing and patenting a wax treatment at the turn of the century to the investment in a state-of-the-art distribution centre at its headquarters at Thorncliffe Park, Sheffield, Ronseal Ltd is recognised as one of the leaders in its field.

"Professionals and DIY enthusiasts alike know they can rely on our products to deliver the results they are looking for," says Kate, "and that they provide a finish that will last."

The foundations for this thriving company, currently employing more than 250, were laid by T.M. Fowler in 1896. His son, T.H. Fowler went on to establish Ronuk Ltd after transferring the business from a small factory in London to Brighton where the fast-expanding company moved into a new factory in 1902 after outgrowing its first home.

Why Ronuk? "There was a competition to rename the business and the winner came up with Ronuk, a Hindu word for brilliance. An early example of smart branding!" says long-time employee and company historian Trevor Pierrepont.

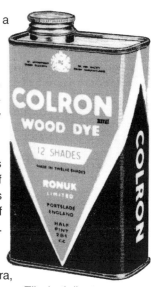

By the 1920s Ronuk was producing a wide range of polishing and cleaning products and was given a royal seal of approval by Edward VII in 1907. More warrants were granted by monarchs of the time, George V, Queen Alexandra, George VI and Queen Elizabeth II.

The company was going from strength to strength and in 1927 what was to become one of the firm's most popular lines, Colron wood dye, was introduced. The brand, which retains its original style of packaging, has been in demand for a remarkable 85 years. The Ronseal name was established in 1956.

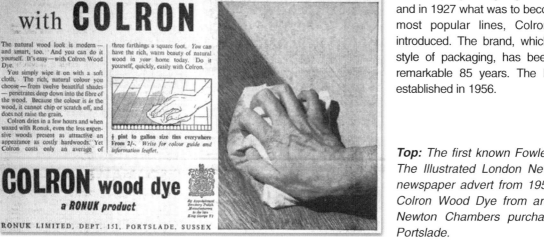

*Top: The first known Fowlers advert placed in The Illustrated London News. **Left:** A Colron newspaper advert from 1957. **Above:** A tin of Colron Wood Dye from around the time that Newton Chambers purchased Ronuk Ltd of Portslade.*

Four years later Ronuk was acquired by Sheffield firm Newton Chambers. Partners George Newton and Thomas Chambers had made their name smelting and casting iron and went on to pool their skills as businessman and craftsman to set up a factory at Thorncliffe where they produced a disinfectant made from distilled coal tar under the brand name, Izal. The company remained heavily involved in iron and steel founding as well as producing chemicals which formed the basis of a range of products manufactured by its Izal subsidiary.

For a short time after its acquisition, Ronuk continued to operate from Brighton but the business was growing and in 1964 the decision was made to construct a purpose-built factory at Thorncliffe to house the Ronuk, Colron and Ronseal production plants as well as one for the Izal arm of the business.

By now, the DIY market was thriving and it soon became clear that the long-term future of the company lay with the Colron and Ronseal brands. The family name, Roncraft, was adopted and launched in 1968 with the two household names forming the cornerstone of Izal Ltd's newly-formed sales division.

Demand for Newton Chambers steel products was starting to fade and was being propped up by the profitable Izal business. "This was the early 1970s when the gas storage manufacturing and oil-fired central heating industry was in steep decline," says Trevor. "Almost inevitably after 180 years of trading independently the Newton Chambers business was acquired by the holding company, Central and Sheerwood."

Top left: Ronseal Floor & Wood Seal from the late 1950s. *Top right:* Some of the first chemists to work at the new Izal-Ronuk laboratories. The picture taken on 23 September, 1960, shows, from left to right, David Bottomley, Graham Mellows, Fred Farrell, John Shaw, John Francis and cleaner, Vera Ridley. *Left and above:* An aerial view of the IZAL-RONUK site in 1972. The block at the top right is the Laboratory block which was converted into offices in 1991, shown above.

A year later the Izal business was sold to the US drugs company Sterling Winthrop and the Chapeltown business was split into three marketing divisions, Sterling Health, Sterling Industrial and the DIY arm, Sterling Roncraft as well as a manufacturing division, Sterling Production.

Sterling Winthrop found the going tough when Government policy ordered hospitals and GPs to prescribe more generic drugs rather than branded products. As a result the three marketing divisions, along with the research and development division relocated to nearby Barnsley while the Chapeltown base remained as a manufacturing site for the products marketed under the Sterling Health, Sterling Industrial and Sterling Roncraft banners.

Unilever acquired Sterling Industrial and Eastman-Kodak bought Sterling Winthrop. Some years earlier the pharmaceuticals' company had bought the Lehn and Fink household products business which included two DIY companies, Thompson and Formby and Minwax. The companies worked closely together and in 1990 Roncraft successfully introduced Thompson's Water

Seal in the UK which quickly created an entirely new market for the DIY business.

Eastman Kodak sold the DIY businesses, including Roncraft, to New York Investment bank Forstmann Little and Co in 1994.

Ronseal Ltd was registered as a company name in 1994 and a year later The Thompson-Minwax Company was formed, a DIY group made up of companies including Ronseal Ltd and Ronseal Ireland - another thriving business based in Dublin.

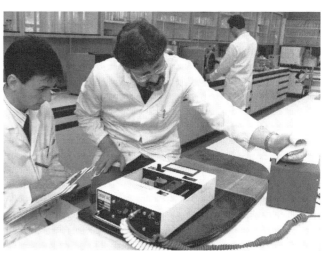

*Top left: Ronseal works personnel regularly held Christmas fancy dress competitions for charitable causes. Picture shows Snow White and the 7 dwarves circa 1981. **Left:** Line inspection on one of the Ronseal products. **Above:** Craig Reaney (Now Ronseal's technical director) and Philip Taylor carry out slip resistance tests on a floor varnish at the newly opened R&D block at Chapeltown. **Below:** Ronseal's automated filling line for Ronseal Fencelife including robotic palletising unit. The line is capable of filling 1,800 5L tubs per hour.*

Thompson-Minwax was acquired by American giant Sherwin-Williams and Ronseal became a subsidiary of its Diversified Brands division.

"The confidence behind the Ronseal brand is illustrated by the significant investment in the Sheffield plant by its parent company," says Trevor.

Ronseal has received funding to modernise the filling and packing area, tank farm. fire prevention and sprinkler systems and in 2007 it invested in a new on-site distribution warehouse which was opened by the chief executive of Sheffield City Council, Sir Bob Kerslake, and Ronseal MD Paul Barrow.

The development was partly financed by parent company Sherwin Williams and the European Union Regional Development Fund.

"The Ronseal name is up there with some of the UK's best-known brands and there is every reason to have confidence in the future," says Kate. "Sheffield is the ideal centre for the business and our commitment to the city gets stronger by the day."

And about that slogan...

Above left: Headquarters of Ronseal Ltd's parent company - the Sherwin-Williams Company, Cleveland, Ohio. *Top right:* Ronseal's new on-site warehouse is clearly visible top left of picture, with adjoining new car parks. *Above:* Ronseal MD Paul Barrow (left) and Sir Bob Kerslake, Chief Executive of Sheffield City Council, officially open the Ronseal Distribution Centre on 15 November, 2007. The Warehouse was partly financed by Sherwin Williams and the European Union Regional Development Fund. *Left:* Ronseal's famous strap line from a TV advert – "Does exactly what it says on the tin". *Below:* An articulated lorry carrying the Ronseal livery, 2007.

Ronseal's "Does exactly what it says on the tin" advertising slogan originated in a series of TV ads first shown in 1994 and is still being broadcast. Created by Liz Whiston and Dave Shelton of ad agency HHCL in collaboration with Ronseal's Marketing Director Ged Shields, the slogan was designed to emphasise that the contents deliver what it says on the tin - that they would act and last.

The expression became widely used - it's one of PM David Cameron's favourites - and last year was voted third in the list of the most quoted advertising lines.

Abbey Forged Products
A Long Tradition

Despite the wider decline of the South Yorkshire steel industry it's not all been gloom and doom in Sheffield. Certainly not for Abbey Forged Products Ltd, which unlike many other businesses has been 'forging ahead' in recent years.

The company is one of Europe's leading metal forging and stainless steel suppliers, with a large metal stock and short lead times on product manufacturing. Abbey Forged Products continues to invest in the latest steel manufacturing technology. This investment is combined with the traditional skills of Abbey's experienced team to provide a truly exceptional service.

Despite rapid growth, however, the values of this family-owned company based at the Beeley Wood Works, Beeley Wood Lane, Sheffield, remain constant - listening as a small team and responding with the capability of a large company.

In excess of 2,000 tonnes of raw material stock are held in an extensive range of grades enabling the company to provide rapid delivery times for bespoke forgings. All raw material is sourced from a small number of European mills with an exemplary quality record.

All elements of the manufacturing process take place on Abbey's own production facility allowing total control of all aspects of production. The workforce has grown to around 200 employees to cope with increasing demand, in particular within the quality assurance team as a response to the increasingly stringent requirements of the industry.

The primary focus is on the provision of bespoke Open Die and ring rolled forgings for the Oil and Gas market with particular emphasis on Duplex, Super Duplex and Nickel Alloy grades. The current weight range covers from 1- 4,000 kgs.

Recent years have seen approvals from, for example, NORSOK, Statoil, BP, Cameron and Exxon Mobil which has assisted in furthering the ambitious growth strategy of the company.

But where does this thriving firm have its roots? The answer is to be found in the mid-19th century.

In 1869, Henry Burkinshaw started in business by opening his own blacksmith's forge.

The business expanded into general forgings using tilt hammers and re-located to premises at Beeley Wood Forge near Hillsborough, in Sheffield, in 1896. Forging at this location dated as far back to 1749 when it was then occupied by the Nova Scotia Tilt Co.

High speed and Tungsten based hot-work steels; Tenax: Cold work, shock resisting and Chromium based hot work steels; Admiral: Austenitic and Martensitic Stainless qualities.

The company experienced steady growth and through the period of the Second World War held 'protected employment' status.

During the 1950s, Pickerings identified a niche area in the manipulation of specialist steels being developed at the time for the ultra-high vacuum industry. It started by supporting areas of pure physics research in universities and dedicated research laboratories. This involves the generation, propagation, measurement and control of nuclear particle beams. The beams were contained in a virtually-total vacuum to eliminate unwanted contamination and steered round the confines of a particle accelerator by super conducting magnets. Observations and measurements taken when these beams collide or impact with prepared targets are at the heart of fundamental physics research.

Facing page: Views of Beeley Wood Forge Circa 1900. **Left and below:** Later views inside the forge.

Henry's son, Wilfred, joined the business shortly after the move to Beeley Wood Forge. In 1902, they moved premises again to Bath Steel Works, formerly the Philadelphia Corn Mill (established in 1843) on Penistone Road, in Sheffield. The move was necessitated due to the requirement for a clean water supply for the newly acquired steam driven hammers.

Wilfred Burkinshaw Ltd was established in 1921, and at the same time Wilfred's son Edward joined the business. Edward was to become a feisty hands-on Director who would run the forge until his death in 1984.

The forge itself had a relatively small weight range, with a maximum forging weight of 100kgs. In 1923 the family formed a new separate company, Pickerings, to develop sales of the forged products produced by Wilfred Burkinshaw Ltd. The new company represented an attempt to get away from the peaks and troughs caused to Wilfred Burkinshaw as a result of fluctuations in the trade cycle, and by the nature of the business which they had traditionally undertaken - hirework forging for the local trade.

Pickerings developed and produced its own types and brands of steel with appropriate trademarks. They were Dreadnought:

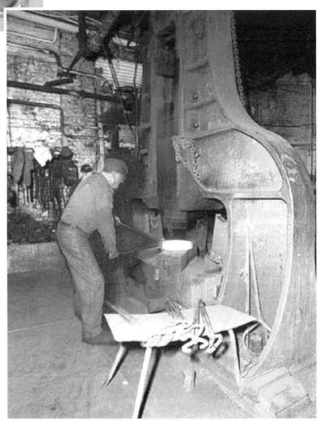

The material developed to meet these criteria was Electro Flux Refined 316LN and was primarily tailored to the requirements of the Conseil Europeen pour la Reserche Nucleaire (CERN) founded in 1952. CERN operates the huge 27km particle accelerator and its associated experiments in Geneva.

Pickerings became a direct supplier of machined forgings to CERN.

Techniques developed at this cutting edge of pure scientific research have spread to the commercial world in areas such as medical radio therapy and super-thin-film technology for semi-conductors and computers. This allowed an industry to develop by exploiting these new processes.

Pickerings became a supplier to many other companies operating in the UHV area and for many years it has been the only UK company stocking and forging EFR 316LN.

As other aspects of the business declined over the years this area became the main source of turnover for the group as a whole.

With the takeover by Abbey Stainless Steels in 2004 new investment and technical upgrades enabled the company to continue and expand on its direct supply status at CERN and retain its unique position as sole UK supplier of this material to the UHV community.

Meanwhile, Edward Burkinshaw had two sons, the fourth generation of the family: Eric the eldest (who was a medical man and a JP) became Chairman until his death in 1987. The second son, Wilfred, ran the forge after his father's death. Wilfred was a hands-on man like his father and even well into his sixties would work on the hammer himself when short handed. He remained with the company until its purchase by

Abbey Stainless Steels, in 2004. Abbey Stainless Steels, founded in 1982, is a company wholly owned by the Neal family who are actively involved in the day-to-day running of the business.

Initially, Abbey Stainless Steels had traded as a steel stockholder, but over the years it began to focus on the supply of forgings to the oil and gas, power generation and nuclear industry. To provide these products the company developed strong alliances with a network of sub-contract suppliers, one of which was Wilfred Burkinshaw's forge.

In 2004, Abbey was approached by Wilfred as a potential buyer for the Group as he was close to retirement and there were no members of the family wishing to join and carry on the family business.

Abbey purchased the Burkinshaw group of companies and proceeded to invest heavily in modernising the facilities. This applied particularly to the forge, which had suffered from a severe lack of investment and had experienced a steady decline. The forge itself looked not too dissimilar from its inception in Victorian times with its cobbled floor and dark cramped surroundings, and required a high level of investment

Top: Staff take a well-earned break to have their photograph taken, 1990. **Left and below:** *Forging today.*

in both new equipment and recruitment of additional forgemen to ensure it could handle the level of work which Abbey was able to provide.

In 2007, Abbey made the decision to move the current business based on two sites to a much larger six-acre facility which had just come onto the market. By an incredible coincidence this site was the same Beeley Wood Forge site where Burkinshaw's forge had been based at the turn of the previous century.

The move was hastened due to the floods of 2007 which wrecked the forge at the Bath Steel Works and resulted in severe disruption for several months until the new forging operation was fully up to speed.

With all operations, forging, metal-testing, heat-treatment and machining, now on the one site, and with continued major investment in all areas of the business, Abbey is proud to be continuing to expand on the steel heritage of Sheffield.

The experienced team at Abbey represents many years in the industry. The company's reputation for integrity and reliability owes much to a committed workforce, producing high quality metal forgings, supported by qualified and accomplished personnel.

In October 2011, the company changed its name to Abbey Forged Products Ltd to better reflect the breadth of products now supplied to original equipment manufacturers (OEMs) around the globe.

Above: An Interior view of Abbey Forge Products' Beeley Wood Works. *Below:* A bird's eye view of Beeley Wood Works prior to recent developments. The view today would be a little different with the addition of new office block and new ring mill, plus the extended heat treatment and test house facility.

Pyramid Carpets - Covering the Years

Pyramid Carpets, based in Crown House, 709 Chesterfield Road, Woodseats, may not be quite as old as the Pyramids in Egypt, but it still has an impressive pedigree with well over half a century of experience in flooring.

Led by Christopher Steer and his son Mark, the firm specialises in providing top quality floor coverings. The company has supplied and fitted carpets and vinyl floor covering to the Copthorne Hotel, Sheffield, and the new Doncaster and Rotherham football stadiums. The firm is currently working in partnership with Sheffield City Council and Rotherham Council on all their floor coverings.

Just after the end of the Second World War Chris's father, Clifford Steer, left the Army and set up in partnership with his brother-in-law. They ran a stall on Chesterfield Market, before moving their small business to Sheffield's Sheaf Market. Despite the difficulty in getting stock in that era of post war shortages, the fledgling business flourished.

Chris Steer recalls his early start in the trade when, at the age of seven, he helped his father sell carpets on

the market in Chesterfield. By the time he was 12 Chris was working on Saturdays as the tea-boy.

Many readers will still recall times when fitted carpets were all but unknown, when lino was the usual floor covering, with a carpet square occupying the middle of the front room. Bedrooms were a different matter: how many of us remember those freezing cold pre-central heating days, getting out of bed and putting our bare feet on the freezing lino instead of the rug?

And who can forget trying to fit that old lino: how easily it used to crack if it was bent too much. 'Lino' is short for linoleum. Lino was made by impregnating rough hessian fabric or waterproof felt with a mixture of oxidised linseed oil (the 'linoleum'), resins such as kauri gum and various fillers before printing a pattern on the resultant sheets. A big marketing point when lino was first sold was that it would

Top left: Mark, Cliff and Chris Steer. **Left and above:** Two examples of the company's commercial flooring contracts. **Below:** Pyramid Carpets' new wood and designer flooring department.

help in the campaign against TB - it could easily be wiped clean after a TB sufferer had finished coughing. Today, vinyl is even more easily cleaned, and ten times easier to fit - and happily TB has ceased to be a selling point!

Fitted carpets only began to make a big impact in the 1960s. Before then, carpets were far too expensive for anyone to think of cutting them to shape. And besides, we wanted to take them with us when we moved. When Clifford Steer started in business few would have ever thought that they would ever be able to afford fitted carpets.

Clifford Steer died in 1997, though not before witnessing the opening of the 1,200 sq ft showroom at Crown House, an addition to the firm's smaller shop in Sheffield's Exchange Street.

Chris Steer then managed in partnership with his sister, Win McHugh (who retired in 2010), and son Mark. Mark deals with contracts together with contracts manager Paul Howard. Terry Dawson (Chris' brother in law) together with Bradley Scholey, deal with the retail department. Chris' wife Jill and daughter Claire Foulstone deal with the firm's accounts.

In 2003, following the refurbishment of Crown House, including a new glass fronted extension, the Exchange Street shop closed. A warehouse at Halfway Sheffield was opened to store the huge range of stock.

Most recently, a new homewares department, including lighting, mirrors and clocks, has opened, together with a new wood/designer flooring department, and a new rug department.

Thousands of commercial floorings have been completed over the last decade, including schools, hotels, stadiums, offices and apartments. Meanwhile, Pyramid's Contract division has grown from strength to strength.

Pyramid Carpets is still a family firm, with Mark and Chris Steer continuing to oversee the day-to-day running of the business.

As well as family members, the company has 15 retail sales staff, and 15 of its own fitters. The firm also employs five teams of contract fitters, whilst for major contracts the firm enlists the service of a dozen sub-contractors

It's all a far cry from those early days on Chesterfield Market.

Top: An overview of Pyramid Carpets' Chesterfield Road premises. **Above left:** *Pyramid vehicles ready to carry out home visits.* **Above:** *Lighting, mirrors and clock in the homewares department.* **Below:** *An exterior view of Pyramid Carpets in 2012.*

University of Sheffield - Learn and Teach

The University of Sheffield's coat of arms features an open book at its centre, on which are inscribed the words 'Disce Doce' - Learn and Teach. There has certainly been a lot of both learning and teaching going on. In 2011, the University of Sheffield was named UK University of the Year in the Times Higher Education Awards.

Judges said that the University 'stood out as a result of a strategy based on its values and rooted in its founding principles' and praised its 'determination and grit' in focusing on the local community.

University of Sheffield is one of the UK's leading universities, with official assessments confirming a reputation as a centre for world-class research. Research partners and clients include Boeing, Rolls Royce, Unilever, Boots, AstraZeneca, GSK, ICI, Slazenger, and many more household names, as well as UK and overseas government agencies and charitable foundations. International academic partnerships include Worldwide Universities Network (USA, Europe and China). A partnership with Leeds and York Universities (the White Rose Consortium) has a combined research power greater than that of either Oxford or Cambridge.

The University developed from three local institutions: the Sheffield School of Medicine, Firth College and the Sheffield Technical School.

The School of Medicine was founded in 1828. Firth College was one of a group of university colleges developed out of the Cambridge University Extension Movement. Mark Firth, a local steel manufacturer, established the College in 1879 for teaching Arts and Science.

Established in 1884, the Sheffield Technical School was the product of the need for better technical training, particularly in steel-making. In 1886 the School moved from Firth College to new premises on the site of the old Grammar School at St George's Square. In 1897, the three institutions were amalgamated as the University College of Sheffield. On 31 May, 1905, the University of Sheffield was granted its Royal Charter.

During the First World War courses were available in munitions-making, medical appliances design and production, translation and politics. In 1919, when returning ex-servicemen were admitted, student numbers rose to a short-lived peak of about 1,000. By then the Faculty of Applied Science had split into Engineering and Metallurgy, the University's first Hall of

*Top left: The University of Sheffield's coat of arms. **Above:** The University buildings in 1905. **Below left:** The first year Chemistry laboratory before its transfer to the new building in 1953. **Below:** Views of the library, completed in 1959 (upper and lower left) and the new Information Commons building (upper and lower right).*

The University also saw a major expansion of its science and engineering facilities with the development of the new North Campus. The hub for multi-disciplinary science and engineering features two prestigious centres, the Kroto Research Institute and the Nanoscience and Technology Centre. The University's Student Village, based at current Endcliffe/Ranmoor sites, provides state-of-the-art accommodation for students. New and refurbished buildings at the old Jessop Women's Hospital provide the latest facilities for some of the University's Arts and Humanities departments.

Residence (the original Stephenson Hall) had been established, and the Edgar Allen library had opened.

The University was equally committed to non-degree teaching; courses included cow-keeping, railway economics, mining and razor-grinding.

The Second World War brought with it new areas of research and training - for example, radar, chemicals, magnetism, naval cartography and glass manufacture.

Post-war, many houses were brought into academic use and new buildings constructed - the Main Library in 1959, and the Arts Tower, Hicks Building, Alfred Denny Building, Sir Robert Hadfield Building, Chemical Engineering Building, University House, five Halls of Residence and the Union of Students in the 1960s.

New buildings for Geography and Psychology followed in the 1970s, along with the Crookesmoor Building (for Law and Management) and the Royal Hallamshire Hospital. The following decade saw the opening of the Octagon Centre and the Sir Henry Stephenson Building for engineering.

In the 1990s, new premises for the School of Clinical Dentistry and the Management School were acquired. The Regent Court building, which houses the Departments of Computer Science and Information Studies and the Sheffield Centre for Health and Related Research, were also completed. In 2007 the spectacular £23 million Information Commons building opened.

Today, the mile-long campus now stretches almost unbroken from St George's Square into Crookesmoor. For the first fifty years of its existence the University's full-time student population did not rise above 2,000. Unsurprisingly, the University now draws students from all over the world to Yorkshire. There are now nearly 25,000 students from 128 countries, and over 5,500 staff – all them keen to both 'learn and teach'.

Top left: *Three generations of University architecture: the original 1905 building was joined by the Arts Tower in 1965 and the Howard Florey building for Biomedical Science in 2004.* *Above:* *In 2007 Vice-Chancellor Professor Bob Boucher received the Queen's Anniversary Prize Gold Medal and Scroll in recognition of the University's contribution to the study of ageing and to improving the quality of life for older people.* *Below:* *The University's new English Language Teaching Centre which opened in 2010.*

Hadee Engineering
Fabrication, Welding and Machining Specialists

Hadee Engineering Co Ltd is one of Sheffield's most highly-respected engineering firms. The business began in Chesterfield in 1969, formed by Robert 'Bob' Almond and Kenneth Dunn. A. D. Engineering, as the firm was originally called, operated from a rented unit on the Storforth Lane Industrial Estate. During that first year the present owner, Peter Lowe, joined.

In his earlier life Bob Almond had been a salesman for a well-known fabrication company in Chesterfield, Pathe Engineering. Before joining the firm, Peter Lowe had been the MD for a Sheffield fabrication company, Swerco Welding Services.

The present company was formed in 1970, by which time Kenneth Dunn had left the business. The firm would now be known as Hadee Engineering Co. Ltd.

Hadee Engineering soon had to find larger premises, which it did in 1971, moving to the old British Rail goods shed on Station Road, at Renishaw.

Following the Markham pit disaster of 1973, Hadee was contracted to supply and fit Cage Catch Gear on all collieries in the north Notts area.

The company continued to prosper, expanding both its premises and workforce. In 1976, it purchased purpose-built premises on its present site at New Street, Halfway, now known as Holbrook.

Meanwhile, Hadee continued to enjoy success and built a 10,000 square feet extension there in 1978.

The company decided to broaden the base of its business from fabrication to also offer design and machining facilities, thus becoming able to offer clients a full service from design through manufacture, installation and commissioning to a full turnkey service.

In 1979, there were still just three employees, but by the 1990s the company would have grown to employ over 100 staff.

In 1988, founding partner Bob Almond, decided to retire. Peter Lowe, bought out his partner's share of the business.

Around 1990, the company embarked on another extension of 10,000 square feet and installed new heavy cranage.

Top: The Hadee Engineering site in 1976. **Left:** *Peter Lowe and Tony Blair at the official opening of the Civic® pilot plant, July 2002.* **Above:** *A 120 tonne electric arc furnace manufactured by Hadee on its way to BSC, Tinsley Park.*

In 1998, Hadee expanded yet again with a further 22,750 square feet extension, which incorporated additional welding and paint spray equipment, together with an extensive yard area to enable larger and heavier engineered products to be built.

The company purchased another site of approximately 1.5 acres in 2005 to ensure that it has adequate land available to grow the business further in future.

Peter Lowe's son Nigel was brought into the business at the age of 16, in 1988. Today, Nigel plays an important role in the operation of the company together with Lee Gordon, his brother-in-law, who runs the machining side of the business.

Other key figures in the company's history include Tim Knight, who joined in 1972 as Company Accountant and worked for Hadee until his retirement in 2010. Anne Almond, Bob's wife, also worked alongside Tim in the early years of the company.

The company prides itself on employing people straight from school and awarding engineering apprenticeships.

The current labour force has mainly developed from apprenticeships and a significant proportion of the management, staff and tradesmen have at least 25 years' service with the company, giving clients the benefit of a wealth of experience.

Current General Manager, Steven Sparrow, Works Foreman, Ian Barker, Purchasing Manager, Peter Quinn, Site Manager, William Weston, Chief Design Engineer, John Marshall, Planner, Andrew Staton and

Expeditor, John Hinchcliffe, have all worked for the company for more than 25 years, together with the secretary/receptionist, Teresa Pickering.

When Hadee was originally established there were thriving coal, steel and foundry industries. However, with their decline new markets have had to be found in addition to the traditional steel industry served in Sheffield such as arc furnaces, steel ladles, scrap baskets, steel furnaces and numerous spare parts.

Large fan casings and a wide variety of spare parts have been supplied to the power generation industry. Hadee is a supplier of main drive gears for both the nuclear and defence industries.

Hadee supplied wing jigs for the largest commercial airliner, the Airbus 380, together with the handling equipment. The firm also supplied and installed the largest dry dock gates in the UK. No fewer than five lock docks were supplied and installed at the 2012 London Olympics site. In Cambridgeshire, Hadee was the supplier of a road-laying manipulator for a Guided Busway.

From its small beginnings four decades ago Hadee has today become an important player on Sheffield's industrial stage.

Top left: *A dragline bucket crane base fabricated at Hadee.* *Left:* *A 350 tonne capacity hook manufactured by Hadee Engineering.* *Above:* *A bespoke worm wheel designed and manufactured through Hadee's in-house design facility.* *Below: A bird's eye view of Hadee Engineering.*

Brook Bakery
Born & Bread on the 4th of July!

Brook Bakery, in Shiregreen, Sheffield, was bought by John Emes in 1988. He began trading on the 4 July that year and still occupies the same location today.

Having started his working life retailing bread, John decided to cut out the middle man and try his hand at making bread himself.

The shop had been a bakers/butchers shop for some time, but when John first took on the rundown business with its five staff, it had just one wholesale customer and very little retail sales.

John soon learned the trade, baking the bread and confectionery with a baker in the back of the shop which still had a butchery department.

Word soon got around about the quality of the goods at Brook Bakery. Other local businesses started buying from the firm to sell its products in their own shops and businesses.

As the bakery got busier John's mother, Eileen Emes, helped out in the shop as well as sometimes helping him with

confectionery. As a result, the bakery's reputation grew. John's father, Jack Emes, also helped out after work making pastry cases for the following days' tarts as they kept everything as fresh as possible – Jack did this even after he retired in 1997 from his job as a lorry driver before he sadly passed away in September 2000.

Brook Bakery now bought a van and John started delivering in between baking. As the round grew a part-time van driver was taken on to deliver around the local areas.

In 1990, the double garage behind the shop was extended and converted into a new bakery, doubling production space.

Next, the 1960s-looking butcher/bakers shop was re-fitted as a modern bread/sandwich shop with a fresh, clean, hygienic feel and cut away from butchery to concentrate on bread and confectionary which was fast becoming the bulk of the business. John was very proud of what had been achieved and

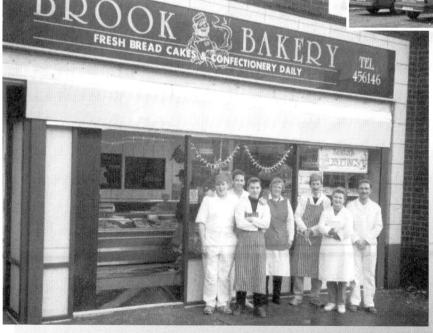

Top: Where it all began, Brook Bakery, Shiregreen, in the early years. *Left:* The team photograph taken after the shop re-fitting in the early 1990s. John can be seen on the far right with his mum, Eileen, on his right. *Above:* The Julian Road, Wincobank, premises when purchased in 1994.

had a team photograph taken outside the shop to mark the occasion.

Business was good and John had lots of plans and ideas to move the business forward. It was, however, getting more and more difficult to fit everything in – John was working and baking six days a week! This led John to bring on board his sister, Susan Gravill, nee Emes, in 1992. She came from an office background and took on the invoicing/accounts/wages role leaving John to get to grips with everything else.

In 1994, the firm received a major blow: the Council wrote saying it was "mass manufacturing in a residential area" and gave John six weeks to either stop selling wholesale or move.

Having pushed the business forward for so long and taken on the required staff to cope, John and his team pulled out all the stops and, not wanting to move far away from their customers, found a unit two miles away on Julian Road, in Wincobank.

Work started on a new 22,000 sq ft purpose-built bakery that was just a shell. It took six years to complete, adding new machinery as they went along. Every penny made was reinvested, with most of the work being done by John and his family. The outcome was worth the wait: on the 12 March, 2012, another chapter opened for Brook Bakery.

The firm now has a fleet of six vans delivering to wholesale customers around Sheffield and Rotherham, four retail shops (the fourth opened on Pot House Lane, Stocksbridge in January 2010), and 50 staff. And it's still growing!

Today John, Susan and Eileen can still be found working at Brook Bakery.

Above left: Construction of the confectionery room. **Above:** *The newly completed confectionery room.* **Below:** *Brook Bakery's shop in Middlewood Road, Hillsborough.*

The new premises were eight times the size of those at Hartley Brook Road. They were fitted out at great expense, but the bank backed the business which pushed on again.

Additional, customers were soon found, and by 1999 the adjoining building was purchased. An even larger bakery was formed by combining the two, creating a 4,500 sq ft work area.

The business now opened more shops, first on Hatfield House Lane, Shiregreen, and in 2003 on Middlewood Road, in Hillsborough.

With bakery shifts starting to overlap and production at a maximum even larger premises were needed. These were found in 2005 - an old ice cream factory 200 yards from the existing site.

Bolton Surgical
Pride Precision Performance

Bolton Surgical Ltd. is one of the largest independently owned surgical instrument manufacturers in the UK. Based in the north of the city, the company is a 'preferred supplier' to both the NHS and private sector hospitals throughout the UK and abroad, with a buoyant, expanding export business to countries such as Saudi Arabia, Kuwait, Egypt, Indonesia and Australia. But where did all begin?

'Bolton Surgical Ltd.' began life in 1936 as 'W. H. Bolton, Scissor Maker'. William Henry Bolton (the great-grandfather of the current Chairman Peter William Bolton), worked throughout the 1920s and early 1930s for J. Gibbins & Sons of 124 Moore Street, Sheffield, a firm of pen, pocket, table knives and scissor manufacturers.

William Henry then left J. Gibbins & Sons and went to work for John Watts of Burnt Tree Lane. It was whilst working there that William Henry saw a business opportunity and started renting a small workshop at the back of 32 Carver Street in the centre of Sheffield.

There, with the help of his son, William Seedhouse Bolton, William Henry worked part-time in the evenings manufacturing surgical instruments such as scissors, artery forceps, sterilising forceps, and bullet forceps (the latter finding a ready market during that period of time).

Prior to the advent of stainless steel in the early 1940s, most surgical instruments were made from carbon steel, and then nickel-plated to protect them from corrosion during the hardening process. Instruments were quenched in whale oil until this became difficult to obtain during the late 1930s and early 1940s.

William Henry was by now manufacturing for the government, and due to high wartime demand the time came for him to leave John Watts and begin running his own business full-time.

During the Sheffield blitz of 1940 many buildings on Carver Street were destroyed, with just a few left standing. The only damage 32 Carver Street suffered however, was a broken light bulb.

Not everyone was so lucky. Most of Bolton's products were manufactured on machines powered by a 2.5 horse power single phase electric motor, which was originally used to power a potato rumbler which was salvaged from a bombed out fish and chip shop on the corner of Burgoyne Road and Bloor Street. Mr. Stringfellow, the shop owner was still in bed when the side of the building was blown away; the only thing left that was salvageable was the motor!

In 1942 the business moved from Carver Street to larger premises at 26 Eyre Lane, Sheffield. The firm now employed nine staff (some full and some part-time). William Seedhouse now worked for the business full-time.

The firm of William Henry Bolton Scissor-Maker, was now exporting to the Dental Company of Toronto, Canada, and supplying many trade customers throughout the British Empire.

Peter William, the grandson of William Henry, having undertaken an Instrument Fitter's Apprenticeship with William Skidmore, took over the joint running of the business in 1982 with his father, William Seedhouse.

The company was re-incorporated as Bolton Surgical Services Ltd. and added instrument repair and maintenance services to its portfolio.

Today Bolton Surgical Ltd., as the business is now called, operates out of a purpose-built manufacturing base in the north of the city. The premises also house the Sales/Finance and Warehousing facilities.

On the solid foundations created by William Henry Bolton, the business has built a reputation for first class superior quality surgical instruments. The company now supply from a range of over 3500 individual products, a far cry from the handful of products initially produced by William Henry in his small 'shop' on Carver Street.

The company still use traditional manufacturing techniques, alongside the technology one would expect from a 21st century leader in surgical instrument supply. The company also operates a highly popular instrument repair and maintenance service in the UK, processing many hundreds of instruments through its Sheffield factory every week, sent in by both NHS and private sector hospitals from throughout the UK and Ireland.

For Bolton Surgical, standing still is not an option: the company's ethos of continuous improvement has helped it keep its place as one of the preferred suppliers in the UK and throughout the world. By responding to and exceeding the needs of its customers both in the UK and worldwide, the business is itself still a perfect instrument for future success.

Top, facing page: The founder, William Henry Bolton. **Bottom left, facing page:** *A view of the old workshop on Eyre Lane.* **Above:** *Charnley Initial Incision Hip Retractor, one of Bolton's top selling products.* **Below:** *Bolton Surgical's premises, 2012.*

ACKNOWLEDGMENTS

The publishers would like to sincerely thank the following

for their help and contribution to this publication

Members of staff at Sheffield Archives and Local Studies Library

Mirrorpix